# Traveling Man's Best Friend

# Traveling with Man's Best Friend

A Selective Guide to California's Bed and Breakfasts, Inns, Hotels and Resorts that Welcome You and Your Dog

By Robert P. Habgood
and Dawn A. Whiting

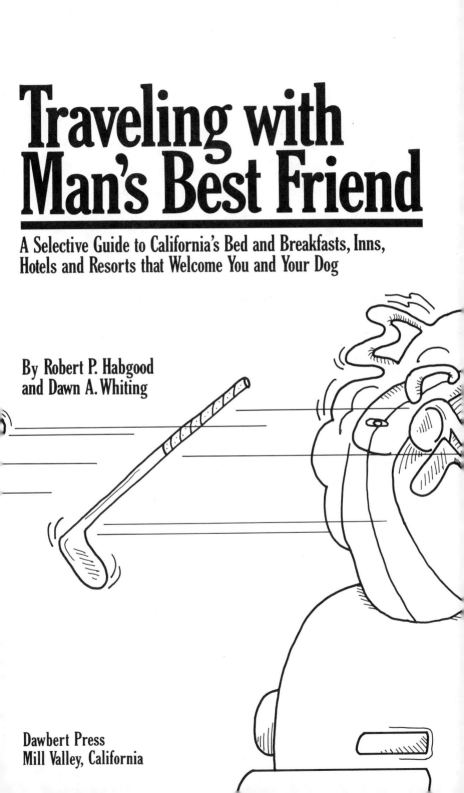

Dawbert Press
Mill Valley, California

Dawbert Press, Inc., May 1985
Copyright © 1985 by Dawbert Press, Inc.

For information address:
Dawbert Press, Inc.
P.O. Box 546
Larkspur, California
94939

COVER DESIGN: Cindy Frost

ILLUSTRATIONS: Lisa Beerntsen

EDITORS: Holly Cronan and Neal Delaporta

ISBN 0-933603-16-9

# CONTENTS

# INTRODUCTION

Americans love their dogs, that is a given. We spoil them with endless amounts of love and attention, and shower them with gifts. The result is terrific companionship. Should you decide to take your pet on a short trip, however, it quickly becomes apparent that what you have, at best, is a difficult proposition. Most places simply do not accept dogs. Long weekends, special vacations, and even spontaneous overnight jaunts are, as a result, almost impossible to organize. Must dog owners resign themselves to making compromising accommodation selections or traveling without their canine companion?

During a recent trip through England, we noted that dogs were accepted additions to most restaurants, inns, and bed and breakfast homes. Unlike their American counterparts, Europeans have mastered the art of bringing along their dogs whenever they travel. It seemed very clear that these little critters were indeed made welcome. Upon returning to California, our task appeared to be quite clear: to locate and describe the unique accommodations which welcome your furry friend. Most importantly, the selected establishments would have to be clean and comfortable, attractively decorated and furnished, and in many instances luxurious and intimate. Moreover, we thought it very important that you and your dog should have plenty of "things to do" during your stay.

"Traveling with Man's Best Friend" will give you the opportunity to forget about those usual problems that arise when you are forced to leave your dog behind:

1.  Boarding your dog in a kennel. (When upon your return, "puppsy" puts you through the guilt wringer for a week or so).
2.  Asking your friends to take care of him or her. ("Please......it will only be for a couple of days......really, he's almost house broken........thanks!")
3.  Sneaking him or her in and out of the hotel room. ("Honest....there's really nothing in my suitcase.....Oh, the tail...uh....)

After many expeditions throughout California, we were able to compile a diversified guide of the inns, bed and breakfasts, hotels, and resorts, which cordially welcome your dog. Some of these fine establishments have special size requirements for their visiting dogs, while others will accept everything from a toy poodle to an overgrown St. Bernard. One standard request of most managers is that when you call to make reservations, please inform them of your traveling companion. They might also ask you a few simple questions about your pet (is he/she small/large, destructive, or housebroken?). Please be honest. A "bad" dog (obnoxious or a constant yipper) can quickly ruin your stay and the manager's pleasant temperament.

Please remember, the innkeepers are under no obligation to accept your dog. They indicated they have welcomed dogs in the past, had positive experiences, and will welcome them in the future, provided the prospective "guests" are extremely well-behaved. It is, of course, up to you as the master and pet owner, to be very considerate and responsible.

We trust this guide will be imformative and helpful, and hope you will truly enjoy traveling with your dog as much as we do with ours.

# TIPS FOR THE TRAVELING DOG

BEFORE YOU LEAVE:

Just as you would plan to bring along certain items or clothing on a trip, your canine companion also has traveling necessities to ensure that he/she is comfortable.

The following is a list of items you should bring when vacationing with your dog:

THE THINGS TO BRING:

* A leash and collar with identification tags.
* A few favorite toys, chew bones, treats, etc.
* A container of fresh drinking water.
* Food and water bowls.
* Dog food, can opener, and a spoon.
* Your dog's bedding (towel, mat, or pillow) or travel crate (kennel) if appropriate.
* Grooming aids (comb, brush, or flea powder).
* Prescription medication - if your dog is currently on any medication, or is a nervous traveler, you should consult with your vet prior to departure.
* As an added precaution, bring all current vaccination records in case of an emergency.


WHILE TRAVELING:

* Do not permit the dog to interfere with your driving. A good place to keep him/her is in the back seat or, in some cases, in a travel crate (kennel).

* Plan frequent stops (every two hours or so). During these breaks you should leash your dog so that he/she does not disturb others, run away, or wander into the road.
* If you must leave your dog in the car, please take the following precautions:
    1. Try to park your car in the shade.
    2. If you have to leave your dog for a long period of time, please check on him/her occasionally.
    3. WARNING: A car acts like an oven and can reach temperatures in excess of 100 degrees very quickly. Prolonged intense heat can cause severe brain damage, and in some instances, result in the death of your dog. PLEASE LEAVE YOUR CAR WINDOWS OPEN ENOUGH TO PROVIDE AMPLE VENTILATION.

ARRIVAL AT YOUR DESTINATION:

We have provided you with a unique selection of interesting bed and breakfasts, inns and resort hotels which will welcome your dog. To further ensure a pleasant visit, we thought it appropriate to include some of the "pet" concerns expressed by managers and innkeepers:

* Your dog should be leashed while on the grounds.
* Do not leave your dog alone in the room.
* Please remember to walk your dog away from the grounds.
* At night, please use the dog's bedding to keep him/her more comfortable and lessen the chance of damaging the furniture.

# REDWOOD EMPIRE

From Arcata to Mendocino

# REDWOOD EMPIRE

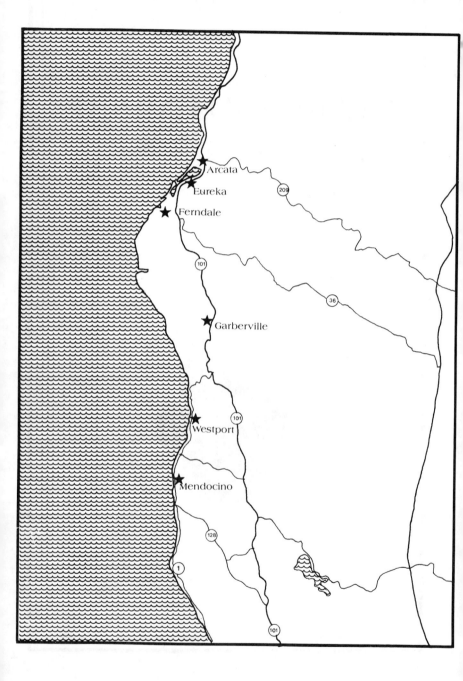

# PLOUGH AND STARS COUNTRY INN
## Arcata

INNKEEPERS:   Melissa and Bill Hans

TELEPHONE:   (707) 822-8236

LODGING:   Seven rooms

RATES:   Double: $38 - 57.
No credit cards accepted.

A trip to the north country would not be complete without a visit to the town of Arcata and The Plough and the Stars Country Inn. This grey farmhouse is nestled on two acres of land, where you can listen to the crickets' songs in the evening and to the roosters' crow in the early morning.

Each of the bedrooms is very unique. There is the private Camellia Room, decorated in rose and pink. Adjacent to that is the largest room (some might call it a suite), furnished in every hue of blue imaginable with views of the expansive fields. A third room, just off the common area, completes the first floor.

Collectively, the two second floor bedrooms, sitting room, and bathroom are ideal for four friends. The "stenciled room" is our favorite, modeled after a similar chamber the Hanses saw in Scotland. The painted floors are hand-stenciled with wreaths, with a single vine painted around the white walls. It is a simple, but effective, touch. The charming decor in the Morris Room completes this very homey inn.

A full Continental breakfast is served each morning in the inn's warm country kitchen. For those with heartier appetites, the Hanses will cook a complete breakfast for a small additional charge.

Whether it be after breakfast, in the middle of the day, or late in the evening; you will want to spend time in the inn's charming living room. Unwind next to their fireplace with a good book, take a crack at one of the many board games, or converse with the other guests. Your host's warm hospitality and the inn's natural charm will make you feel right at home.


PUPPY POLICIES: The Plough and the Stars will accept your dog provided you give them plenty of advance notice. More importantly, the Hanses also have a friendly family dog. If the two do not get along, however, yours will have to sleep in the car.


FRISKY FRIVOLITIES:
   * A trip out to the jetty, guarding the entrance
     to Eureka Bay, is always fun. Here you will

4

find a long beach for running the dog, and on a good day, pounding surf. (Caution: the undertow is treacherous; look but do not leap.)

* The inn is located in farm country. If you and your dog like to jog/walk or bicycle, this is an excellent area for scenic explorations. (very flat).
* Sequoia Park is a 52 acre grove of redwoods, ideal for long walks. It also contains a zoo, duck pond, and wandering herds of deer and elk.

PEOPLE PLEASURES:
* Visit the Arcata Marsh and Wildlife Sanctuary (located at the Base of "I" Street).
* The Samoa Cookhouse (built in the 1800's) is a local institution, being the only cookhouse left in the West. The museum is interesting enough, but the draw is the food - all you can eat and reasonably priced. This is truly a wild dining experience: (707) 442-1659.
* The Caspar Hot Tubs provide you with a fine excuse to relax after a long day of exploring: (707) 964-6668. Children under 7 are free.

THE PLOUGH AND THE STARS COUNTRY INN, 1800 27th Street, Arcata, CA., 95521.

# EUREKA INN
## Eureka

MANAGER:       John E. Porter

TELEPHONE:     (707) 442-6441, (800) 862-4906

LODGING:       150 rooms and suites

RATES:         Single: $45 - 52,
               Double: $52 - 68,
               Suite: $95 - 225.
               Credit Cards:  All Major.

The Eureka Inn first opened its doors in 1922, after 600 investors came forward and funded the construction of this four-story Tudor hotel. It was renovated in the mid 1960's, and today the distinctive high beamed redwood design, unique guest chambers, and well manicured lawns, give this retreat a charm all of its own.

Upon entering the lobby, guests cannot help but be impressed with the massive English candle chandelier, huge fireplace, lush carpeting, and beautifully carved French doors which lead out to the garden and pool. For those who wish to enjoy a special holiday trip, we highly recommend a visit to the Eureka Inn. Every year the inn hosts an extravagant "White Christmas" celebration complete with a 25 foot tree, decorated with anything from 2000 live orchids to 15 pairs of beautiful white doves. Whatever the occasion, you will find the inn allows you the opportunity to step back into historical Eureka.

After a long day exploring Humboldt county, you may wish to utilize the inn's pool, sauna, spa, or jacuzzi. Afterwards, relax in your cozy room which could be decorated in any number of ways, ranging from a conservative red and blue motif to a royal gold and navy blue combination. Many of the rooms have exposed redwood moldings, while others boast a lively or traditional colonial printed wallpaper. A few of the featured amenities include color television, refrigerator, and historical prints of Eureka. Guests also have a choice of queen- or king-size beds, and views of either the pool and gardens or downtown Eureka.

You need only walk downstairs to enjoy some of the finest dining in town. The inn's Rib Room offers a wide selection of Humboldt Bay seafood specialties, and a varied Continental fare. After dinner, guests may wish to listen to the nightly piano player "tickling the ivories" in the lounge.

PUPPY POLICIES: The Eureka Inn welcomes your furry "little friend" without charge or damage deposit.

FRISKY FRIVOLITIES:
* Enjoy the wilderness surrounding Blue Lake, where you may catch fish, or observe their various stages of growth at the Mad River Hatchery (on Hatchery Road).
* Visit the Fort Humboldt State Historic Park, a mostly restored 1850's military post where U.S. Grant was stationed. There is also a museum that features exhibits of the logging, railroad, and military history of the area.
* Visit the 106,000 acre Redwood National Park. (It is so gigantic it has been broken down into smaller state parks!) Here you will find hiking trails, redwood forests, and rushing rivers for canoeing and kayaking.

PEOPLE PLEASURES:
  * Visit the Sequoia Park and Zoo (over 52 acres of redwoods).
  * A short car trip to Scotia will bring visitors to the Pacific Lumber Company, one of the largest operating lumber mills in the world.
  * Take a walking tour of Old Town in Eureka. There are beautifully restored Victorian mansions and many quaint shops (which will relieve you of several dollars) to help you capture the area's special flavor.

EUREKA INN, 7th and F Streets, Eureka, CA., 95501.

---

# GINGERBREAD MANSION
## Ferndale

INNKEEPERS:  Wendy Hatfield and Ken Torbert

TELEPHONE:   (707) 786-4000

LODGING:     Four guest rooms

RATES:       Double: $45 - 65.
             Credit Cards:  MC and VISA.


The Gingerbread Mansion lies in the heart of Ferndale, a town that has come to be known as the "Victorian Village". Ferndale is impeccably clean, the lawns well-manicured, and the village store fronts beautifully restored. This civic pride has prevailed since the mid-1880's. Wendy Hatfield and Ken Torbert, in keeping with these traditions, have provided an elegant Victorian setting for the guests of the Gingerbread Mansion.

From the outside, the mansion looks slightly intimidating, but this feeling disappears as you walk through the leaded glass doorway into a cozy foyer. High ceilings, loads of family antiques, period pieces, and other goodies fill every corner of the hallway, living room, library, and dining room. As a result, each guest chamber is equally as warm and inviting as the next.

In keeping with this mood, the bedrooms have been painstakingly decorated using soft, floral wallpaper and light colors. The oversized beds with stuffed pillows and intricately carved wooden headboards are just a couple of furnishings that help to set this Victorian theme. The most unique room has a private porch, and occupies an entire corner wing of the mansion. The beauty of this guest room is reflected in a mirrored ceiling, while the warmth is generated by a Franklin stove.

The two bathrooms, one upstairs and another

downstairs, are shared by the guests. (Your hosts even supply you with bathrobes for braving the short trek down the hallway.) This shared bath experience is rather special though, as you will find the upstairs bathroom is spacious enough to comfortably accommodate 20 people. This room is magnificent; the highlights are the ball and claw bathtub (in the center of the room), a mirrored ceiling, and murals of vines and flowers adorning the walls. It is so luxurious that you might find it difficult to leave.

But leave you must, because tea is served in the parlor from 4 p.m. to 6 p.m. If you miss tea, then the Continental gourmet breakfast will more than make up for this lost experience. You will dine on incredibly tasty baked goodies during both breakfast and afternoon tea. Your host's gracious hospitality will perfectly complement this grand experience.


PUPPY POLICIES: Understandably, dogs are not allowed in the mansion; however, there is a small enclosed gazebo just outside the front door (on the front porch) that would be a cozy spot for a very well-behaved dog. Advance reservations must be made for your dog (please bring his/her bedding).


FRISKY FRIVOLITIES:
* Ferndale is just minutes from the ocean. The beaches are long and the surf is rough.
* Downtown Ferndale is three blocks from the Gingerbread Mansion. The streets are wide, the houses ornate, shops antiquated, and the people are very friendly. In June, the local children dress their pets in fine clothing and show them off at the annual pet parade.

* Russ Park is only a few blocks away. This is a beautiful bird sanctuary, intended for the true nature lover.

PEOPLE PLEASURES:
* Each year there is a wild Kinetic Sculpture Race. This race is run over land and water and attracts the most bizarre and ingenious contraptions you have every seen (held June 24-27).
* The shopping in Ferndale is truly your "best bet". Merchants have selected very unique items for their clientele. You are sure to find something for that difficult person on your gift list.
* The 85th Annual Humboldt County Fair and Horse Races is a tremendous crowd pleaser. Rooms are booked a year in advance for this August event. If you are lucky enough to be in town for the occasion, please attend: (707) 786-9511.

THE GINGERBREAD MANSION, Ferndale, CA., 95536.

11

# BENBOW INN
## Garberville

INNKEEPERS:   Patsy and Charles Watts

TELEPHONE:    (707) 923-2124

LODGING:      56 rooms, deluxe rooms with fireplaces, and a cottage suite

RATES:        Twin Bedroom: $75,
              Queen/king bedroom: $58 - 95,
              Deluxe king bedroom: $115 - 125,
              Deluxe fireplace king: $150,
              Garden cottage: $190.
              Credit Cards: MC and VISA.

The Benbow Inn is a large four-story English Tudor Mansion that, after opening its doors in 1926, changed hands so many times it soon fell into disrepair. However, during the inn's early heyday, President Herbert Hoover, Mrs. Eleanor Roosevelt, Charles Laughton, and John Barrymore were some of the more notable guests. In 1978, the Wattses came to the rescue of this historic landmark and spent several years restoring the inn to its original grace.

The lobby, with its high ceilings and a huge stone fireplace, contains an assortment of antique clocks, Oriental rugs, and carved wood furniture. As you meander up the stairs, take special notice of the warm cherry-wood wainscotting and thick, plush carpeting in the hallways. All of the inn's bedrooms have been completely refurbished and redecorated. They are now filled with impressive antiques, and comfortable beds adorned with floral coverlets, complemented by matching wallpaper and draperies. The views from your bowed windows, of the rushing river and surrounding valley, will surely tempt you into taking a leisurely stroll about the grounds.

In 1983, Patsy and Chuck tore down all of the riverside quarters, replacing them with very spacious guest rooms. These deluxe bedrooms, on the garden and terrace levels, are definitely the most appropriate for you and your furry friend. The decor is primarily a country motif, that is perfectly complemented by beautiful antiques, wood burning fireplaces, and private terraces/patios. The Garden Cottage even has its own jacuzzi and wet bar. Some other personal touches include a decanter of red wine, a basket of mystery novels, and (in deluxe rooms) an exotic selection of fruit juices.

Each day at 2 p.m., patrons are invited to attend a traditional English tea, complete with scones. You will then need a brisk walk to make enough room for the evening hors d'oeveres. If you should miss this gastronomical delight, fear not. Patsy and Chuck will not let you go hungry, as their gourmet dining room features a host of appetizing entrees such as roast duckling, filet mignon, and milk fed veal.


PUPPY POLICIES: They will gladly accept your canine cohort. Please telephone the Wattses in advance to let them know you are both planning a visit.


FRISKY FRIVOLITIES:
   * They dam the local Eel river until it becomes

a lake. This provides an appropriate spot for your dog to practice his/her dog-paddle.

* Claiming to be one of the "world's finest", the Rockefeller Forest features redwoods that reach an estimated 350 feet. There is a large rearing tank for steelhead as well as a lumber museum on the premises.
* Hiking, fishing, and picnicking on the river are pleasant ways to spend your afternoon. The surrounding valley is perfect for long nature walks or bicycle rides.

PEOPLE PLEASURES:
* Scotia is the site of the largest redwood lumber mill in the world. The daily tour is fascinating and well worth a special trip.
* Ferndale: (several miles down the road) is an immaculate town filled with restored Victorian houses and stores that transport the traveler 50 years into the past.
* Explore the "Avenue of the Giants" - a scenic drive through the oldest redwood forests in the world.

THE BENBOW INN, 445 Lake Benbow Drive, Garberville, CA., 95440.

# HOWARD CREEK RANCH
## Westport

INNKEEPERS:  Sally and Sunny Lasselle

TELEPHONE:  (707) 964-6725

LODGING:  Seven rooms in cabins and a boathouse

RATES:  Double: $35 - 65.
No credit cards accepted.


    Alfred Howard first built the Howard Creek Ranch in 1872 and it later became a stage coach rest stop. Located just three miles from the quiet little village of Westport, the ranch commands a scenic view of the ocean and long sandy beach. Guests are sure to enjoy the natural beauty and serenity of this sprawling, grass valley.

The two original redwood houses, connected by steep New England-style roofs, form one long main house. This farmhouse is filled with dozens of American antiques and all sorts of interesting collectables. To this day, the original fireplace still heats the parlor and other guests' quarters. In the outbuildings, visitors are able to choose from a wide range of accommodations. Would you like to relax on a private balcony, or do you wish the light, airy sensation of skylights and lofts; perhaps a kitchenette is what you desire. All of these amenities are available at the ranch. Each room contains a sink, and if you would prefer to cook, kitchen arrangements may be made with your hosts. The two remaining accommodations are the cabin and boat house, which both have electricity and wood burning stoves. The boat house is the converted hull of an abandoned boat, complete with a galley kitchen. The special features in this unique guest quarter are the large picture window overlooking the river and handmade quilt adorning the bed.

A delicious breakfast of coffee, fresh fruit, eggs, and bread/muffins is served as soon as the guests begin to migrate to the dining room. This is also the site of the late afternoon wine or beer tastings, supplemented with assorted "munchies".

The ocean is available for swimming, but most find it more appropriate for perspective members to the "Polar Bear Club". Therefore, you will most likely decide the swimming pool, set along the hillside, or the wood-heated hot tub is your best bet. In either case, a therapeutic moment or two in their sauna will surely rejuvenate any aching muscles. In addition to the outdoor activities, you may enjoy "tinkling the keys" of their organ or piano. Best of all, this unique retreat provides a perfect combination between a natural ocean setting and a charming country inn.


PUPPY POLICIES: Sally and Sunny gladly welcome your canine companion to the ranch. They greatly appreciate your advance "doggy" reservations.


FRISKY FRIVOLITIES:
* Explore the surrounding fields in the valley and stroll down the sandy beach at low tide. There is an abundance of wildlife, not to mention the migrating whales, in the area.
* Westport is a small town, reminiscent of old New England. Wandering through this quiet village and other Mendocino county towns will prove interesting.
* The Westport-Union Landing and the coastal beaches are terrific locations to surf cast and hunt for your fill of abalone.

PEOPLE PLEASURES:
* The Coast Range Preserve consists of 4,000 acres of wilderness. One of the beautiful and interesting places to stop is the Elder Creek Basin: (707) 984-6653.
* Laytonville lies in the heart of an old lumber region and redwood forests. This is a great place for hunting and fishing, particularly in the Eel River Valley: (707) 247-3318.
* The Skunk Train (a standard gauge railroad) chugs along from Ft. Bragg to Willits. During the course of its journey it passes through massive redwood forests and over the Noyo River: (707) 964-6371.


HOWARD CREEK RANCH, P.O. Box 121, Westport, CA., 95488.

# AGATE COVE INN
## Mendocino

INNKEEPERS:   Joan and Tom Johnson

TELEPHONE:    (707) 937-0551

LODGING:      9 cottages

RATES:        Double: $69 - 99.
              Credit Cards:   All Major.

The Agate Cove Inn was built in the 1860's and strives to maintain the simple charm of days gone by. Your hosts, the Johnsons, wish to make you "comfortable, relaxed, and well fed, so your stay will be a memorable one". They accomplish just that by providing spacious guest cottages, large hearty breakfasts, and a serene, picturesque environment.

Each of the cottages is named after a semi-precious stone (Garnet, Topaz and Jasper) and perhaps you will think of them as "gems" as well. They are individually decorated utilizing a country decor to set the theme. The handmade quilts on each of the four poster or canopy beds contain a plethora of bright colors to complement the scenic surroundings. You may nestle under your quilt while enjoying a crackling fire (in your Franklin stove) or watching the ocean crash against the craggy cliffs. A complimentary bottle of wine will further warm those who still feel an early evening chill. A great deal of attention has also been given to your private bathroom, for it is spacious and luxurious.

Each morning you will awaken knowing that your appetite will be fully sated by Joan's gigantic breakfast feast. This begins with freshly brewed coffee or tea, homemade baked bread, fresh jams, and a huge omelet that is filled with your choice of ham, cheese, mushrooms, chilies and/or sausage. Moreover, you may either watch your omelet being concocted on the old wood stove or marvel at the spectacular ocean view from your breakfast table.

PUPPY POLICIES: The Johnsons welcome your dog at the inn. They do request that you inform them in advance of your pup's visit, and that you not leave your "friend" alone in the cottage.

FRISKY FRIVOLITIES:
* Mendocino is filled with many historically interesting architectural relics, that house fine art galleries and stores. You will relish the beautiful walk to town (about 1/2 mile).
* The Headlands State Park is an excellent area for a pleasant stroll with your dog, providing incredible views of the rugged California coastline. (Note: You may wish to leash your dog as the cliffs are very steep.)
* Several local beaches close to the inn are perfect places for running or partaking in an early morning dip with your furry companion.

PEOPLE PLEASURES:
* This is a terrific area to explore either by bicycle or on horseback. You may even wish to venture through the Russian Gulch State Park to visit the waterfalls, redwood forests, and a magnificent sculpted promontory: (707) 937-5804.
* The underwater park at the Van Damme State Park is an excellent location for skin-diving.

If catching fish seems more entertaining, then casting for steelhead in the Ten Mile River will prove more rewarding.
* Visit the Redwood (some reaching 300 feet) or Pigmy (mature trees that are only 2 feet tall) Forests just off of scenic Highway 1.

AGATE COVE INN, P.O. Box 1150, 11201 North Lansing Street, Mendocino, CA., 95460.

# BIG RIVER LODGE
## Mendocino

INNKEEPERS:    Joan and Jeff Stanford

TELEPHONE:     (707) 937-5615

LODGING:       23 rooms and suites

RATES:         Double: $80 - 96.
               Credit Cards: AE, MC, and VISA.

Tucked into the dramatic cliffs and gigantic pine trees of Mendocino, the Big River Lodge is the perfect retreat from a hectic world. This two-story, redwood lodge is perched amid a lovely flower-strewn clearing, well off the road. All of the guest rooms have faded wood decks looking out over the crashing Pacific ocean.

The Stanfords have tried to anticipate almost all of their guests' needs by providing a varied selection of books, decanter of red wine, and hand dipped chocolates in each room. The inn is very homey, and this can be attributed to the ambitious efforts that have gone into selecting the fine country antiques, local artwork, and warm colors for the furnishings. For those who crave a touch of the modern, the Stanfords have included remote control color television, individually controlled thermostats in the bedroom, and heat lamps and Waterpick shower heads in the bathroom. There is one secret we have not disclosed – each room has a wood burning fireplace. Now, what more could you ask for?

A Continental breakfast is presented every morning in the reception nook. Take a moment to look at all of the goodies your hosts have collected over the years. There are teddy bears in every corner, interesting antiques, and informative books on the Mendocino area. We visited at Christmas time and found a beautiful tree decorated with handmade ornaments and a train running circles around its trunk.

Whatever the season, rest assured, your stay at the Big River Lodge will be most memorable.


PUPPY POLICIES: Your four-legged friend is warmly welcomed at the Big River Lodge, provided he or she is leashed when on the property.

## FRISKY FRIVOLITIES:

* There is a beautiful beach, just a few minutes from the lodge, for your dog to romp across and/or dig up.
* The lodge also rents canoes (Catch A Canoe) to take out on the Russian River for either a picnic or day trek. (This is obviously not for dogs who have an strong aversion to water.)
* Visit the Mendocino National Forest, where you will have over 1 million acres to explore (but don't do it all in one day). There are a variety of recreational activities for those who truly enjoy the outdoors.

## PEOPLE PLEASURES:

* The lodge will let you borrow their bicycles. A ride to the town of Mendocino should only take a few minutes - the rest is left to you.
* The Forest Service offers walking tours of Jughandle State Reserve. You can observe the various geologic phenomena, as well as the famous pygmy forests.
* If skin-diving, bicycling, and fishing are of interest to you, then the Van Damme State Park is worth a visit.

THE BIG RIVER LODGE, P.O. Box 487, Mendocino, CA., 95460.

# WINE COUNTRY

Napa, Sonoma, and the Russian River

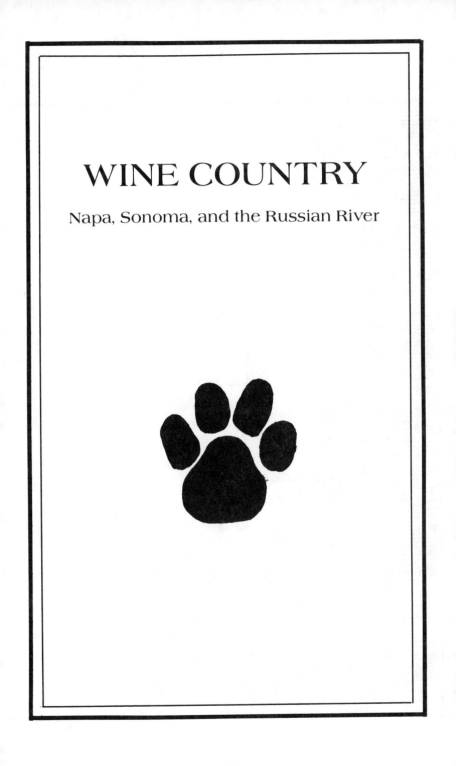

# WINE COUNTRY

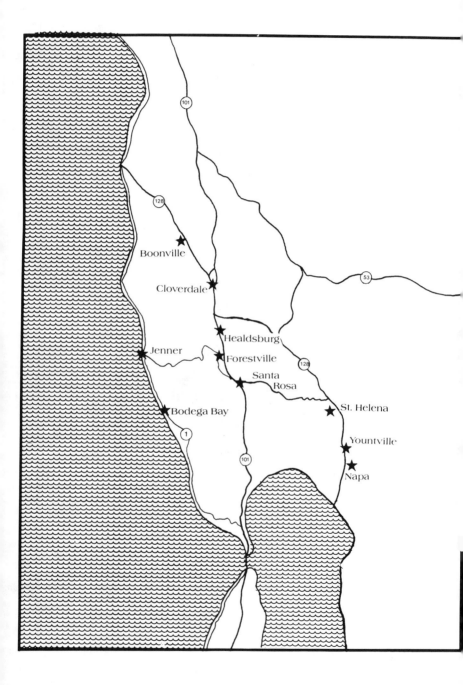

# BEAR WALLOW RESORT
## Boonville

INNKEEPERS:  Bob and Roxanne Hedges

TELEPHONE:  (707) 895-3335

LODGING:  7 cabins and 1 suite

RATES:  Cabin: $65 - 85,
Suite: $50.
Credit Cards: MC and VISA.

    The Bear Wallow Resort is located just four miles from the scenic town of Boonville, in the heart of the vineyard-laden Anderson Valley. The huge lodge and scattered cabins were built in the 1960's, yet they retain the simple, rustic nature that "city folk" yearn for when visiting the woods. Upon arriving at the lodge, you will soon become entranced by the coolness and majesty of the oak and redwood, and refreshed by the scent of pine from the nearby forests.

Once inside the lodge, you will be greeted by the animal welcoming committee. This entourage consists of the Hedges' two setters and the lodge's mascot, an enormous stuffed bear who resides in a chair next to the piano (daring you to "tickle the the ivories"). If rest and relaxation are what you seek, then ask Bob to fix one of his famous liquid concoctions from the intimate bar. (If he is not available, you may take advantage of the "Honor Bar" system where you keep track of your drinks on a napkin.) With drink in hand you may enjoy "kicking back" and letting the day slip by in front of the forty-foot fireplace. Ah...but you say you want a little exercise, then stroll out onto the stone porch or one of the other decks and watch the sun dip into the western sky.

Now that you are fully at ease, it might be time to stroll over to your cottage. Each is truly a forest hideaway, out of sight (and earshot) of your neighbors. Whether you are residing in the Eagles Nest or Mountainair, you will discover your cottage to be a "home-away-from-home" with its fully-equipped kitchen, living room, dining area, and either one or two bedrooms. Special touches such as country antiques, colorful bed quilts, and fresh flowers give your accommodation a unique charm. Of course, a visit to the country would not be complete without a roaring fire, (in some cases housed in a Franklin stove) and a bottle of sherry to warm your spirits. The exposed beamed ceiling supplies the sensation of spaciousness, while the plush wall-to-wall carpeting, overstuffed sofas, and charming curtains at the windows give the cottage a feeling of coziness.

Unlike traditional bed and breakfasts, guests are self-sufficient when it comes to satisfying their grumbling tummies in the morning. However, at the end of the day, the Hedges will be bustling about the kitchen preparing delicious entrees for dinner. Selections vary from chicken and fresh seafood to barbecued steak and filet mignon.

PUPPY POLICIES: The Hedges have two friendly dogs of their own and gladly welcome "polite pets".

FRISKY FRIVOLITIES:
* A terrific adventure for both you and your dog is to visit the coastal town of Mendocino. Explore the many shops and galleries, and do not forget to take a walk on the Headlands for spectacular coastal views.
* In Boonville you may wish meander along the Azalea Discovery Trail, or frolic with your dog in the Faulkner County Park.
* The Hendy Woods State Park is an excellent area for teaching your "outdoor" dog (or soon to be) the finer points of fishing. You can also wander the dozen or so nature trails that wind through redwood groves:(707) 937-5804.

PEOPLE PLEASURES
* A great afternoon diversion is a visit to a few of the many local wineries in the area.
* This is the heart of the "appleland" and is a perfect spot for taste-testing the various flavors and cross-breeds.
* Enjoy Boonville, a town that is sleepy in comparison to the hustle and bustle you left behind. Visit the Mailliard Redwoods State Reserve, local history museum, and sample the nouvelle cuisine at the Boonville Hotel.

BEAR WALLOW RESORT, P.O. Box 533, Manchester Road, Boonville, CA., 95415.

# THE OLD CROCKER INN
## Cloverdale

INNKEEPERS: Don and Els Kinderis

TELEPHONE: (707) 894-3911

LODGING: 10 rooms

RATES: Room: $50 - 70.
Credit Cards: MC and VISA.

The Old Crocker Inn was originally built in 1897 as a summer retreat for Henry J. Crocker. To this day, through the never ending efforts of the innkeepers, the hostelry maintains much of its original charm. Located near the top of the Asti hills, you will enjoy the seclusion and bucolic setting of the Old Crocker Inn. Even the lodge's guests' rooms share the open-air feeling of the outdoors.

You may choose from guest rooms in either the main lodge or in one of the outlying buildings. Five, spacious bedrooms in the lodge, surround a central courtyard that was originally the site of a swimming pool. These bed chambers are uniquely decorated with throw rugs covering pegged floors, French floral wallpaper, and country antiques. A 12 foot ceiling increases the sense of spaciousness in both the bedroom and large private bathrooms.

The other three buildings contain another five bedrooms, decorated in the same manner as those in the main lodge. In addition, the lodge also contains a rather unique common area. A capacious dining room is paneled in Kauri wood, while the massive brick fireplace warms the oaken living room. Relax in front of the roaring fire with a glass of wine while Don and Els share their stories about spending seven years sailing the waterways off Alaska.

Each morning you will find a complimentary breakfast of fresh fruit, pastries, cheese, and other seasonal goodies awaiting you in the dining room. You may enjoy this in the pool area, under the oak trees, or in the dining room before a large picture window.

You will want to arrive early in the day, and wander around this natural wonderland filled with wild birds, squirrels, Blacktail deer, and quail. You may also wish to "catch a few afternoon rays" by the newly built pool or play a badminton match.

PUPPY POLICIES: Don and Els will gladly accept your fluffy friend. They have two very nice dogs of their own who would love to make new friends.

FRISKY FRIVOLITIES:
  * The inn has acres and acres of fields, filled with local wildlife, for you and your dog to investigate.
  * The towns of Cloverdale and Boonville are interesting side excursions. If you wish to continue the trip, drive further to Mendocino, a charming New England-styled town on the coast. On the way you will also find great beaches for running your furry friend.
  * Enjoy an exploratory excursion through the Hendy Woods State Park (redwood forest) or along the Russian River. Both areas are just down the road from the inn.

PEOPLE PLEASURES:
  * There are more than two-dozen wineries in

the area for your sipping pleasure (especially around Geyserville).

* Paddle down the Russian River in a canoe: the best launching location is in Asti. Ask your hosts for more exact information about the other appropriate spots.
* Visit Calistoga, the home of many hot springs and health resorts. You can also try out the Calistoga Soaring Center for glider rides over Napa Valley: (707) 942-5592.

THE OLD CROCKER INN, 26532 River Road, Cloverdale, CA., 95425.

---

# ISIS OASIS
Geyserville

INNKEEPERS: Lora Vigne and Paul Ramses

TELEPHONE: (707) 857-3524

LODGING: 12 bedrooms in the lodge, 3 Yurts, 1 Barrel room, assorted teepees

RATES: Rooms: $35 - 50.
Credit Cards: MC and VISA.

The Isis Oasis is a complete change of pace from any other inn or bed and breakfast. As soon as you drive onto the grounds, you will notice a small zoo containing everything from a peacock and Egyptian pheasant to emu and ocelot. This animal menagerie is located next to a country farmhouse, painted in rust with a lavender trim. The giant "meditation" tree shades the lush expanse of lawn, separating this area from the open-sided pavilion. This building is the setting for your scrumptious country breakfast and dinner.

The Isis Oasis is truly eclectic, and not for the conventional guest. The accommodations are unique, bordering on offbeat. For instance, have you ever heard of, or stayed in, a Yurt? Well, the Isis Oasis has three of them on the property. A Yurt is a circular canvas tent-like structure with a clear dome on top. It is rustic with no room for a bath, but ample space for a comfortable double bed and antique dresser. Of course if you seek something a bit more unusual in terms of a sleeping arrangement, then try the Barrel Room. Yes, it is an actual wine cask (complete with the subtle essence of Cabernet) converted into a cozy and very private bedroom. Of course, you might also want to sleep as the Indians did, in a teepee.

If these accommodations are not quite what you had in mind, then take heart, for there are 12 individual lodge rooms for your sleeping pleasure. These feature hardwood floors, a varied assortment of country antiques, and double beds covered with subtly colored handmade quilts. Lora has also contributed to the decor of the guest rooms with her handmade stained glass windows and Egyptian artwork.

The eight acres offer something for everyone. The Isis Oasis hosts an exceptional dinner/theatre, and also holds workshops for actors. If you crave rest and relaxation, we recommend reading a good book in front of the lounge fireplace or working on your tan next to the swimming pool and jacuzzi. A sauna, in the converted wine barrel, will sooth your aching muscles, as will the complimentary bottle of wine found in each room.

PUPPY POLICIES: This bed and breakfast gladly welcomes animal guests to their "oasis".

FRISKY FRIVOLITIES:
* You may wish to wander the grounds around the Isis Oasis, hike through the nearby hills (Bradford or Fitch Mountains), or along the 40 miles of trails by Lake Sonoma.
* Take a trip to the Warm Springs Dam and see the fish hatchery: (707) 433-9483. The river is a great spot for fishing and picnicking.
* Take your dog on a journey through historic Geyserville. It is within walking distance of the Isis Oasis, and is a small, but interesting community.

PEOPLE PLEASURES:
* This region is ideal for long-distance canoeing or for a short afternoon paddle. A few local spots worth trying are Healdsburg Memorial Beach and the boat launching spot in Asti. Bob Trowbridge also runs canoe trips: (707) 433-7240.
* The dozen or so Alexander Valley vineyards will give you a diverse sampling of California wines at their finest.
* The bicycling in this valley is outstanding. The roads are flat, the scenery is spectacular and the weather, usually cooperative.

ISIS OASIS, 20889 Geyserville Ave, Geyersville, CA., 95441.

# DRY CREEK INN
## Healdsburg

MANAGER:       Cindy Abilay

TELEPHONE:     (707) 433-0300

LODGING:       103 rooms and suites

RATES:         Single:  $25 - 45,
               Double:  $42 - 62,
               Double/Double:  $42 - 60.
               Credit Cards:  All Major.


The Dry Creek Inn is a white, Spanish-style structure with a large bell tower standing in the center of the facade. Guest rooms are located on three different tiers, with lovely views of a small vineyard, grassy field, or the distant hills. The rooms on the backside of the upper two floors will offer visitors much quieter accommodations, better views, and more privacy. Although, in terms of design, decor, and furnishings, all of the guest chambers are similar.

You will find your room to be quite large and open. The camel-colored carpeting is luxurious, complemented by rich, multi-colored, floral-striped bedspreads covering queen-size beds (a few of the rooms have waterbeds). Naturally finished Danish wood furniture and wine country prints beautifully enhance this decor. A bottle of wine, color cable television, and fresh flowers are just a few of the accoutrements awaiting you. A pair of sinks set in a Normandy rose base lie just outside the very spacious, modern bath.

The lobby is also painted in a soft Normandy rose, with vineyard memorabilia, navy blue sofas, and contemporary furniture serving as the perfect accompaniment. Each morning a full complimentary Continental breakfast is served in this chamber. Many people choose to bring breakfast to their bedroom and enjoy a more leisurely morning. The inn also has a heated swimming pool and spa for enervating early morning workouts or for the late afternoon "floaters" and "paddlers".

PUPPY POLICIES: The inn welcomes your dog and asks only that you do not leave him/her alone in your room.

FRISKY FRIVOLITIES:
* Take your dog up to the Austin Creek State Recreation area, it is located three miles north of Guerneville on Armstrong Woods Rd.
* The Russian River flows right by Healdsburg. You may wish to explore some of it on your own, finding the ideal location for a little sunning, swimming, and good ol' relaxing. A perfect alternative is a visit to the beach in Healdsburg.
* Spend the day wandering through the local countryside. Farmers in the area produce all sorts of delicious goodies, from blueberries and apples, to endive, garlic, and indian corn. Check with the tourist bureau for a free map of the "Farm Trail", that will help you find all of your favorite farm products.

PEOPLE PLEASURES:
* The wine is waiting to be tasted at some of

the good local houses: Pedroncelli, Clos du Bois, and Souverain. A fine guide to the wineries is "California's Wine Wonderland." (Send $.50 to California's Wine Wonderland, P.O. Box 7244, San Francisco, CA., 94120).

* Bicycle along the country roads which wind their way through valleys, vineyards, and alongside the Russian River. A terrific map is available from the Healdsburg Spoke Folk Cyclery: (707) 433-7171.

* The orchards and vineyards all around the Healdsburg vicinity serve as a great excuse for the many special festivals, such as the Blossom Tour, Wine Fest, and the Cloverdale Citrus Fair. Consult their tourist bureau: (707) 433-6935.

DRY CREEK INN, 198 Dry Creek Road, Healdsburg, CA., 95448.

---

# MADRONA MANOR
## Healdsburg

INNKEEPERS: John and Carol Muir

TELEPHONE: (707) 433-4231

LODGING: 14 rooms and two suites

RATES: Double: $75 - 95,
Suite: $115 - 140.
Credit Cards: AE, MC, and VISA.

The Madrona Manor was built in 1881 by John A. Paxton to be used as his family's summer home. Over a century later, the Muir family arrived and began the extraordinary restoration of this historic landmark. As you drive through the massive gate guarding the manor's eight wooded acres, you will feel as though you are visiting a chateau in the French countryside.

Each of the manor's bedrooms is individually decorated with beautiful antiques, large carved headboards, four poster beds covered with antique quilts, huge dressers, and floor-to-ceiling tie-back curtains (this is quite effective as the ceilings are 14 feet high). The rooms each have ornately tiled fireplaces and bathroom sinks are bedecked with brass fixtures and marble tops. The intricately woven Persian rugs are scattered throughout the house, completing the warm and cozy atmosphere the innkeepers have so carefully nurtured.

The Carriage House used to be just that - an old stable for horses. Look for the small, original windows throughout the house. During your visit you also might inquire about the extensive work that has gone into the refurbishing of this historic landmark. The Carriage House guest bedrooms are furnished with a more contemporary flair. The simple decor is very comfortable but does not have the same elegant ambiance found inside the manor. On the first floor you will find a pool table and assorted board games in a cozy sitting room.

There is also a "honeymooner's cottage" set apart from the rest of the buildings. This has a sitting room, bedroom, and a small private deck off the back, overlooking a lovely garden. The bathroom "throne", oddly enough, is the cottage's focal point. Its base is an antique white elephant, and high above your head is the wooden flush box with a long brass cord. The remaining building houses two suites, perfect for families visiting the inn, as they provide complete privacy.

Every afternoon, around 5 p.m., guests are invited into the manor's sitting room for some complimentary wine and cheese beside the antique piano. Do not let this fill you up, as dining at the Madrona Manor is truly a culinary delight. The Muir's three-star restaurant serves breakfast (to the guests of the inn), dinner, and a special champagne brunch every Sunday. The Muirs have installed a smoke house, so they can cure their own meats. The dinner menu features everything from Alaskan king crab and fettuccine to mesquite grilled thresher shark and poussin. All of their meals are cooked with vegetables picked right from their garden, while their preserves are prepared from seasonal fruit. With all of this delicious food, the Muir's hospitality, and these charming accommodations, we are sure you will completely enjoy your visit at the Madrona Manor.

PUPPY POLICIES: The Muir's welcome your dog at no additional charge. We do recommend that you make prior arrangements and keep your little furry friend leashed while on the property.

FRISKY FRIVOLITIES:
* Paddle down the Russian River in a canoe, fish for bass, or search for a secluded picnic spot.
* Hike the trails in the Sonoma and Armstrong Redwood Forests, where you will undoubtedly find buckets and buckets of wild blueberries, strawberries, and raspberries (in season).
* A short drive up the coast gives you an ideal opportunity to look for the migrating whales, fish for ocean salmon, or just dig for clams.

PEOPLE PLEASURES:
- \* Experience the annual Scottish Gathering and Games (Santa Rosa) and the Harvest Hoedown (Healdsburg).
- \* If recreation is the theme of the day, a little swimming in the manor's heated pool or tennis (on nearby courts) may do the trick.
- \* Sample the wares of the local vineyards on your way to one of the music festivals at the Armstrong Woods, Russian River (jazz), and in Guerneville.


MADRONA MANOR, 1001 Westside Road, P.O. Box 818, Healdsburg, CA., 95448.

---

# STILLWATER COVE RANCH
## Jenner

INNKEEPER:    Lynda Rudy

TELEPHONE:    (707) 847-3227

LODGING:      7 rooms in cottages

RATES:        Double:  $29.20 - 65.
              No credit cards accepted.


The Stillwater Cove Ranch sits perched on a knoll overlooking the jagged Sonoma coastline, but lies only yards away from a beautiful, dark, sandy cove. It is a rustic slice of California, a rare and special find in a world of prefabricated buildings and fast food. You instantly know you have come to a unique spot when, upon your arrival, a dozen gorgeous peacocks strut over to greet their new guests.

The accommodations vary, but rest assured, they are all open and airy. The East and West Rooms have picturesque ocean views through the pine and fir trees. Entire afternoons can be spent on the wide porch just daydreaming and listening to the waves crash on the shore. Equally pleasant evenings will follow next to a blazing fire in the stone fireplace. Both of these rooms have full baths, kitchenettes, and two double beds. In the rear wing of the building are the King and Science Rooms which look out over the fields to the forest. The Science Room has a Swedish fireplace, king-size bed, and day bed, while the King Room (has a king-size bed, of course) is a bargain at $29.20 per night.

The Teacher's Cottage is set off by itself. This room is smaller than the others and far more cozy. A pair of double beds set next to the stone fireplace provides a cozy and intimate atmosphere. Finally, there is the Dairy Barn which is for those who like to "rough it". You will discover these accommodations consist of eight bunk beds, two showers, a stocked kitchen, and a rustic wood-burning stove that supplies the heat. Each guest should bring his or her own linens.

PUPPY POLICIES: Your dog is an accepted guest at the ranch. Your innkeeper has even developed a set of guidelines that should be observed during your stay. They are as follows:
* Owners must be in complete control of their dog at all times.
* Please bring bedding for your dog and keep him/her off the furniture, including the beds.

* It is recommended that you take your pup for at least two walks a day - away from the cottages.
* Guests will be charged for any pet-caused damage.
* If your dog is disruptive, the innkeeper will have to ask you to leave.

## FRISKY FRIVOLITIES:

* Walk/run on Stillwater Cove Regional Park beach. Here you may fish, search for shells, or hike on the trails.
* Comb the many acres of trails adjacent to the ranch. We will leave it up to you and your dog to discover the beauty of this area.
* Drive up the coast, pick one of the dozens of picturesque points of land (any point will do), and watch the grey whales during their seasonal migration.

## PEOPLE PLEASURES:

* The Salt Point State Park surrounds the ranch. There are well over 5,900 acres to explore. You may fish, dive for abalone, go horseback riding or hike on the trails.
* Visit the Fort Ross State Historic Park, three miles from the ranch. This is an abandoned Russian fur-trading outpost with stockade, chapel, barracks, and exhibits of artifacts: (707) 847-3286.
* Drive down the coast to Jenner. Swim, hike, paddle, or drive along the Russian River. By the way, this region has an abundance of vineyards, and apple orchards. Stop by and sample some of their products.

STILLWATER COVE RANCH, Highway 1, Jenner, CA., 95450.

# FT. ROSS LODGE
## Jenner

INNKEEPERS:   Karen and Tony Romeo

TELEPHONE:   (707) 847-3333

LODGING:   16 rooms

RATES:   Double: $36 - 72.
Credit Cards: MC and VISA.


The Fort Ross Lodge is set back from the rocky Sonoma coastal cliffs, giving guests a beautiful view of both the countryside and the ocean. These grey-blue wooden buildings face away from the road, and are a welcome sight to the weary traveler.

The cottage furnishings follow a simple theme, with various soft-tone color schemes adding to the comfortably cozy design. Your hosts provide the special touches, such as placing a bowl of fresh fruit and vase of flowers in each of the rooms. These one-room chambers have small refrigerators, and we recommend that a few staples be brought along, if you are planning an extended stay. (In case you forget something, there is a store across the street.) However, if cooking is not on top of your list of "things to do" while traveling, then make a reservation at the Salt Point Lodge (just a few miles down the road) and enjoy one of their fine dinners.

Backgammon boards, volleyball paraphernalia, croquet, and other assorted "toys" are available for the visitor needing a competitive diversion. A perfect way to top off the afternoon is to relax with a couple of friends over barbecued steaks. Best of all is the view of the ocean from your private patio, especially if it is complemented with a blazing fire. Of course, a visit to the north coast is just not complete without a therapeutic dip in a hot tub – the lodge provides this, along with a sauna, for those who wish to fade into oblivion...

PUPPY POLICIES: The innkeepers welcome your dog and charge a $5/night fee.

FRISKY FRIVOLITIES:
* There are endless hiking trails in the local area (ask the innkeeper for more details).
* Enjoy the five beaches located in the vicinity of the lodge. True Californian dogs will love to romp on, dig up, or just "hang out" on one or all these sprawling beaches.
* Walk from the lodge across the cliffs to the ocean. Bring your binoculars and watch for grey whales. There won't be any crowds – just you and your dog.

PEOPLE PLEASURES:
* Just north of the Fort Ross area is Salt Point State Park, where one can fish, go horseback riding, dive for abalone, and hike through some of the 5,970 acres.
* The area surrounding Sebastopol is the center of the apple growing industry for Northern California. It is well worth investigating, particularly in the fall.
* The nearby Russian River offers canoeing, swimming, fishing, and a chance to explore Duncans Mills and Monte Rio.

THE FORT ROSS LODGE, 20705 Coast Highway 1,
Jenner, CA., 95450.

---

# BODEGA BAY LODGE
## Bodega Bay

MANAGER:       Kate Caldwell

TELEPHONE:     (707) 875-3525

LODGING:       64 rooms and suites

RATES:         Double w/kitchenette: $62 - 72,
               Double w/fireplace: $74 - 84,
               Double w/king: $74 - 88,
               Two room suite or a very spacious
               specialty room: $96.
               Credit Cards: All Major.

The Bodega Bay Lodge is ideally situated on
the Northern California coast between the Russian
River and the Tomales Bay - Point Reyes National
Seashore. Each of the guest quarters is designed
to complement the lodge's rustic setting, while still
providing comfortable modern amenities. The oak
beamed ceilings and furnishings, fireplaces, wicker
sofas and sitting chairs, fresh flowers, and woven
baskets of budding plants, are just a sprinkling of
the many accoutrements setting the mood for these
rooms. You may wish to relax on the private patio
or deck, with a cup of fresh complimentary coffee,
as the sun slowly dips into the ocean. Guests will
also enjoy views of the bird-filled marshlands, and
wooded hillsides.

Each morning a delicious Continental breakfast is served in the lobby. While munching on freshly baked goodies and sipping fresh juices, you can watch the many beautiful tropical fish swimming in the two 500 gallon saltwater aquariums.

Afterwards, a stroll through the lodge's many acres is the perfect pastime for those who enjoy exploring a bucolic setting. An ideal way to gear up for the day, is to take a refreshing dip in the heated swimming pool or unwind in the therapeutic hot whirlpool spa (glass enclosed for a panoramic view).

PUPPY POLICIES: The Bodega Bay Lodge charges $5/night for your little friend.

FRISKY FRIVOLITIES:
* There are superb areas to explore with your dog along the Russian River or in any one of the nearby State Parks.
* Visit the restored settlements of Fort Ross and Duncans Mills.
* Ride one of the lodge's bicycles along the country roads or jog on the paths leading to Doran Beach.

PEOPLE PLEASURES:
* Boat charters are available for either deep sea fishing or whale watching. (Bodega Bay houses California's busiest commercial fishing fleet, north of San Francisco.) If you want a close encounter of the first kind with these sea creatures, we highly recommend a visit to the California Bodega Marine Laboratory (at Bodega Head).

* Rent horses from a local ranch and ride down the beach or on the local equestrian trails.
* You might want to practice your golf swing at the Bodega Harbor Golf Course.

BODEGA BAY LODGE, Coast Highway 1, Bodega Bay, CA., 94923.

---

# THE LODGE AT FORESTVILLE
## Forestville

INNKEEPER:    Leo Smith

TELEPHONE:    (707) 887-1556

LODGING:      10 Bedrooms

RATES:        Single:  $79,
              Double Suite:  $89 - 99.
              Credit Cards:  MC and VISA.

The Lodge at Forestville came into commercial existence as a railroad depot, but in more recent years it has been converted to a comfortable inn. Renowned as one of the oldest buildings in Sonoma County, the original lodge houses a restaurant and bar, while the adjacent cottages serve as the guest bedrooms.

The mustard yellow cottages are surrounded by large shade trees. Each one has a wooden gate which opens into a tiny courtyard, leading directly to the sliding glass door of the room. This is a perfect location for your dog as he/she is free to wander in and out of the room, without the danger of straying too far.

Guest rooms are individually decorated with American country antiques including painted iron bedsteads or carved wooden headboards, writing desks, and marble-topped bedside tables. Thick, dusty rose carpeting perfectly complements the delicate floral-stripe wallpaper pattern. The rooms are fairly small, but are quite unique as they each have a whirlpool tub (for two) in the bathroom and a dry heat sauna off the bedroom. From your private spa there is a wonderful view through the picture window of the landscaped hillside. Privacy is one of the key elements at the lodge, ideal for those romantic weekends.

If you wish a bite to eat, a stroll across the way will bring you to the lodge's restaurant. The menu features selected entrees of fresh salmon, beef wellington, and a variety of vegetables (all from their garden). Scrumptious desserts, followed by the lodge's infamous rich espresso, will top off your meal.

A large heated swimming pool, encircled by a dozen small cabanas, is situated toward the rear of the property. Here you will also discover private hot tubs and saunas. After a therapeutic "deep heating", a quick dip in the lodge's frosty running stream will provide the same beneficial treatment that made the European spas famous.

PUPPY POLICIES: Your hosts eagerly welcome your traveling companion.

FRISKY FRIVOLITIES:
* The nearby town of Sebastopol is in the heart of California's apple growing country. If you enjoy watching an apple crush, celebrating at the "Apple Blossom" festival, or just sampling the cider, apple butter, and other goodies, plan on a visit.
* The Russian River is the focal point for those fishing, canoeing, and swimming enthusiasts. While visiting this region, you should also explore the riverside towns of Duncans Mills, Guerneville, and Jenner.
* Armstrong Redwood State Reserve consists of 752 acres, filled with rambling trails. Spend the day exploring the area, or stop by their entertaining outdoor theater.

PEOPLE PLEASURES:
* Investigate the dozens of vineyards on the Russian River Wine Road: (707) 433-6935. Those who prefer the red carpet treatment, may wish to try Laura Salo's special tasting tours complete with gourmet picnics: (707) 538-2338.
* Bodega Bay is the site of Hitchcock's classic thriller, "The Birds". It is also the home of a quaint fishing village, the Marine Laboratory Tours, and Doran County Park.

* Try your hand at paddling on the Trowbridge
  guided canoe trips. These excursions last
  anywhere from 2-7 hours: (707) 433-7247.

THE LODGE AT FORESTVILLE, 7871 River Road,
Forestville, CA., 95436.

---

# MORGAN'S HIDEAWAY
## St. Helena

INNKEEPERS:   The Morgans

TELEPHONE:    (707) 963-3134

LODGING:      One bedroom cottage

RATES:        Cottage: $65
              No credit cards accepted.

Morgan's Hideaway is a quaint little cottage
off the beaten "wine country" track. It lies next
to the Morgan's shingled house, a circular pool set
in redwood decking, and on the edge of a heavily
wooded area. The door to the cottage (set into
the shingled roof) leads to a suite, which will
dazzle you with its exceptionally clever use of
color and light.

A cheery yellow and white sitting room with a
comfortable sofa, overstuffed chairs, and a coffee
table (loaded with magazines and books) welcomes
each guest. After a long day of wandering around
the wine country this is a perfect place to relax,
particularly over a few glasses of sherry from the
decanter in your room. As sleepiness settles in,

you need only take a few short steps to your bed that lies in a charming alcove on an elevated white iron bedstead, draped with a coverlet of small red, yellow, and white flowers. A private bath is just as close. This cottage is a cozy oasis for anyone visiting the St Helena region.

One item that is worth special mention is the delicious breakfast that your hosts prepare and deliver to your cottage every morning. You may enjoy this at a small, intimate table for two, set especially for each guest.


PUPPY POLICIES: The Morgans will gladly accept your canine companion. Please do try to make advance reservations, and most importantly keep your dog under careful watch so he/she does not wander off into the woods.


FRISKY FRIVOLITIES:
* The Bale Grist Mill is a state historic park that is approximately 1 mile north on Highway 29 (on the left).
* The Bothe Napa State Park is a great place to wander around with the pooch or to just find a sunny spot to enjoy an afternoon picnic.
* Explore the quaint towns of Yountville, St. Helena, and Calistoga along the wine country road.


PEOPLE PLEASURES:
* Visit the world famous Napa Valley vineyards. In addition to offering some very tasty wine, several of the vineyards also have outdoor concerts in the summer and fall.
* After shopping in the various local towns, do not forget to stop at the Cement Works for a

unique dining treat and some fun browsing.
* Revel in the natural beauty of the hillsides on
the way to Sonoma. In town you will find a
great old western square that contains many
interesting boutiques and eateries.

MORGAN'S HIDEAWAY, 2951 Highway 29, St.
Helena, CA., 94574.

---

# MIRAMONTE HOTEL
# AND RESTAURANT
## St. Helena

INNKEEPER:    Edouard Platel

TELEPHONE:    (707) 963-3970

LODGING:      2 rooms above a gourmet
              restaurant

RATES:          Double: $71.50.
                No credit cards accepted.

The Miramonte is renowned for its excellent French restaurant; however, there are also two wonderful upstairs bedrooms that the proprietor has renovated and refurbished for his guests. The small inn is located just off the main street of St. Helena, a perfect venue from which to explore the local sights and the entire Napa Valley.

The rooms are nestled above the restaurant overlooking a small courtyard. They are easily accessible through an entrance at the side of the building. A short flight of steps leads you to a private redwood deck. The guests' chambers are simply decorated in a French Provincial motif. Navy - white fabrics adorn the sofa and matching chair in the sitting room of one suite, with a naturally finished oak bureau serving as a fitting complement. The queen bed rests on a platform with pretty, woven baskets hanging from the wall. The second bedroom is also decorated with early American antiques, and contains a double bed, covered with a fluffy comforter.

Adjoining the suite, there is a navy blue tub that is so unique it deserves a further mention. This ball and claw bathtub has been beautifully restored so that the brass legs shine and the oak ring around the rim has a wonderful luster. This chamber has several shuttered windows that will either allow the warm afternoon sun to pour in, or deter any peering eyes. If possible, do make a reservation at the Miramonte's restaurant, their cuisine will definitely enhance your sojourn.


PUPPY POLICIES: The Miramonte asks that you bring your dog up to the guest room through the private entrance.

## FRISKY FRIVOLITIES:

* Take a trip to Lake Berryessa, a mere 20 miles from St. Helena. You will find boating, fishing, and other water sport activities.
* The Bale Grist Mill State Park is an old flour mill with a 36-foot overshot water wheel, first used in 1847.
* Walk your dog through the quaint streets of St. Helena. You will enjoy the beautifully restored architecture while your dog pulls you along to the parks. Yet another pleasant excursion is a hike through the foothills bordering this scenic valley.

## PEOPLE PLEASURES:

* Make reservations to tour Chateau Montelena's vineyard and afterward, picnic on one of the small islands in the lake. To round out this adventure, a stop at the Compleat Winemaker (St. Helena) will enhance your wine making acumen and give you some tips on producing your own home vintage.
* A visit to the Petrified Forest will show you where Mount St. Helena's volcanic eruption uprooted many of the region's redwood trees. Six million years later, visitors are able to see and learn more about these fallen giants.
* Rent a bicycle and enjoy a truly enervating, exploratory bike tour over this fairly flat terrain.

MIRAMONTE HOTEL AND RESTAURANT, 1300 Railroad Avenue, St. Helena, CA., 94574.

# HYPHEN INN
## St. Helena

INNKEEPERS:  Suzanne and Edouard Platel

TELEPHONE:  (707) 942-0434

ROOMS:  Two cottages, 1 suite

RATES:  Rooms: $90.
No credit cards accepted.

Nestled snugly between the hills of the Napa Valley, The Hyphen can truly be called a special retreat. Vineyards, orchards and fir trees surround this sprawling country estate. If you visit in the spring you are treated to the sight of apple and plum blossoms, while a late summer or early fall stay will allow you to sample the apples, plums and grapes that are just being harvested. Any time of year is nice for visiting The Hyphen as it is always a romantic retreat.

Upon your arrival you will most likely be greeted by Suzanne and her five Shih Tzus (yes, count them, five). This entourage will escort you to your accommodations in either one of the two cottages or the suite in the main house. The cottages lie amid lush flowers and greenery. One is decorated in the pink tones and the other in wine country burgundy and blue. Simple, country antiques and carpets are scattered throughout the rooms, with hardwood floors peeking up through them. After a long day in the wine country, you may wish to slip into a hot bath or take a quick shower before relaxing in front of your Franklin stove. The Platels have also left you a decanter of port to toast the end of a full day.

The suite in the massive main house is quite a contrast to the cottages. It is decorated with vibrant white wicker, dazzling your eyes from the moment you enter the room. These chambers are so light and airy that you may just decide to read a good mystery in front of the brick fireplace in your sitting room. On the other hand, if you do need to soothe your tired muscles at the end of the day, there is a luxurious European soaking tub in your private bath.

Each morning's breakfast is truly a pleasure, even if you are not a "breakfast person". Fresh seasonal fruits (berries, pineapple, papaya), and homemade jams and jellies with croissants are tasty treats. Coffee or tea are always available, and if you are very lucky you may even dine on some of Suzanne's "famous" bran muffins or coffee cake.

After a filling breakfast, you may want to go for a swim in the large, solar heated pool. You may want to keep an eye on your "furry friend", as some of Suzanne's other "pet guests" have been known to inadvertently go for a dip.


PUPPY POLICIES: Suzanne loves dogs and she welcomes yours. She prefers females and advance notice.


FRISKY FRIVOLITIES:
* Visit the Napa Valley Olive Oil Manufacturing Company in St. Helena and select some picnic supplies for a wine country adventure. A few local spots for outdoor dining are Lyman and Crane Parks in St. Helena.
* Follow the trail up Mt St. Helena that leads to the Robert Louis Stevenson cabin.
* Perhaps you would like to spend a peaceful morning just wandering over the many acres

that make up The Hyphen's property.

PEOPLE PLEASURES:
* Does candle making intrigue you? The Hurd Candle Factory in Freemark Abbey offers free demonstrations of beeswax candle making. You may even want to purchase some of their wares.
* If you fancy yourself to be a Robert Louis Stevenson fan, then visit the Silverado Museum in St. Helena: (707) 963-3757. This is devoted to the life and works of the late author.
* If you prefer to be totally self-indulgent during your wine country sojourn, then we have the perfect suggestion. Drive over to Calistoga and take a mud bath and a steam, swim in a hot mineral pool, and cool down with a massage at any one of the spas.

THE HYPHEN, P.O. Box 190, St. Helena,. CA., 94574.

---

# THE HARVEST INN
## St. Helena

INNKEEPER:     Richard Geyer

TELEPHONE:     (707) 963-WINE

LODGING:       32 Tudor cottage and manor rooms

RATES:         Double: $85 - 155.
               Credit Cards:  MC and VISA.

The Harvest Inn is a collection of English Tudor style cottages, set just outside the town of St. Helena. It rests on 21 acres of vineyards, in the heart of the wine country. Guests are free to either wander through these vineyards or along the beautifully manicured paths that criss-cross the grounds. Enjoy the fragrant flower gardens, play with a rooster or two, and watch schools of fish swimming in the ponds (your dog will surely find this entertaining).

The chambers are appropriately named after varieties of wine. Please don't let your passion for Cabernet keep you away from the Chianti or Merlot rooms, for each is just as warm and inviting as the next. Brightly woven rugs are scattered over pegged, mahogany stained floors, with fine antiques filling every corner of the room. You will definitely find the fireplace a cozy addition to these charming cottages. Plus, there is more than enough firewood at your disposal.

The innkeepers have created an atmosphere that could be part of another century, but have not neglected the modern conveniences. Guests may choose from a list of amenities which include a queen- or king-size bed, wet bar, kitchen, and full-size private balcony or terrace. The bathroom is fully modernized, with the exception of a copy of an old fashioned "pull chain" toilet. You will also enjoy the am/fm radio and color television in your room. During the summertime a large, heated swimming pool is at your disposal and a jacuzzi is kept bubbly, hot year round.

A Continental breakfast of fresh fruit, pecan and cinnamon rolls, muffins, juice, and coffee is served each morning in the reception area. This common room is truly a masterpiece, dominated by a six foot high, 12 foot wide, brick fireplace. The high, wood-beamed ceilings, pegged floors, and the eclectic combination of antiques will capture your imagination. The multicolored, stained glass windows that look out over the vineyards are also noteworthy. Finally, for those of you who have the afternoon or midnight "munchies", there are jars of peanuts, bubble gum, mints, and freshly popped popcorn to satisfy your cravings.

PUPPY POLICIES: Your dog will be given the royal treatment at the Harvest Inn. There is a modest charge of $5/night. Please keep "Bowser" leashed when wandering the paths.

FRISKY FRIVOLITIES:
* The 21 acres of vineyards are owned by the Harvest Inn. Feel free to walk or jog with your dog throughout the grounds.
* Visit one of the parks in St. Helena. Crane Park and Lyman Park are both good bets.
* Take your dog to the Napa River (follow Pope Street). Stonebridge Park lies at the edge of the river. You can relax in the sun while your dog swims a few laps.

PEOPLE PLEASURES:
* Sample a little of the grape while visiting the wine country. The Beringer Winery is five minutes up the road and offers an informative tour. If there is a particular winery that interests you, ask your hosts for assistance in setting up a special private tour.
* St. Helena is a wonderful town for shopping and observing the many interesting native stone facades. The St. Helena Hotel has a very extensive wine bar, with interesting

specialty stores located around the corner.
* Take an early morning hot air balloon ride over the Napa Valley. Two local companies which provide this service are: "Adventures Aloft" or "Napa's Great Balloon Escape". It can be as elegant or as simple an excursion as you wish.


HARVEST INN, One Main Street, Saint Helena, CA., 94574.

---

## MELITTA STATION INN
### Santa Rosa

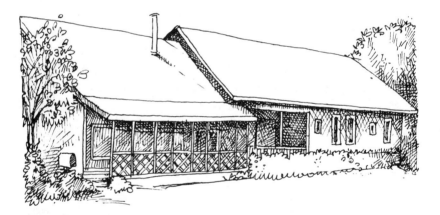

INNKEEPER:    Diane Jefferds

TELEPHONE:    (707) 538-7712

LODGING:      Six bedrooms

RATES:        Room: $55 - 65.
              Credit Card: VISA.

The Melitta Station Inn was originally a 19th century railroad stop, more recently converted into a charming 20th century bed and breakfast. Diane Jefferds has put a tremendous amount of work into designing and decorating her inn, taking care to bring out its natural country charm. The sitting room is magnificient with exposed wood-beams, an old Franklin stove, quilts, dried and fresh flower arrangements, and dozens of woven baskets, of all shapes and sizes, filling the room. Hand stenciled designs line the long hallway, doors, and windows providing a special touch found in few American country inns.

Diane's idea for the inn evolved during an extended European sojourn and subsequent visit to the East Coast. The trips obviously had a lasting effect, ultimately manifesting themselves in the Melitta Station Inn. The guest rooms have either raised iron or wooden bedsteads, covered with antique quilts. French provincial fabrics drape the windows and coverlets, while Oriental and braided rugs cover the hardwood floors. Selected antiques complement, rather than clutter, the room. Some pieces are painted in subtle greens and blues with hand-stenciled flower patterns adorning the edges, others are covered in fabric, and a few are naturally finished.

Most of the rooms have private baths, some with ball and claw tubs, others with tiled showers. Small baskets of potpourri (Diane makes it herself) and sweet-smelling soaps will delight your nose, and handmade baskets and dried wreaths will tickle your fancy.

Each morning you will find a full breakfast awaiting you on the Welsh sideboard. The fare varies from day to day, and choices could include quiche, egg casseroles, muffins, coffee cake, and scones. French doors invite you out to a redwood porch, or if the day is cool, dine in front of the Franklin stove.


PUPPY POLICIES: Your well-behaved lap dog is a welcome addition to the Melitta Station Inn. Please call in advance and talk to Diane about making a "dog reservation".


FRISKY FRIVOLITIES:
* Annadel State Park is only a few "walking" minutes away from the inn. You will find miles of horsetrails, a beautiful lake, and a scenic meadow to romp in.
* Spring Lake is a even closer. A jogging path and bicycle trails run along the perimeter of this man-made reservoir.
* Take your dog to visit Patti the Pig, a 500 pound neighbor of the Jefferds. Patti was quite pregnant during our visit, and perhaps you will be lucky enough to meet her piglets.


PEOPLE PLEASURES:
* Bicycling is the perfect pastime in this area. The roads are flat, the countryside scenic, and the people, friendly.
* Visit the local wineries, starting with Chateau St. Jean, continuing down to Sonoma. This area is rich in fine wines and heritage.
* Drive over the mountains to Calistoga and spend the day in a mud bath, mineral pools, and natural hot geysers.


MELITTA STATION INN, 5850 Melita Road, Santa Rosa, CA., 95405.

# NAPA VALLEY LODGE
## Yountville

INNKEEPER:   Ellis Alden

TELEPHONE:   (707) 944-2468

LODGING:   55 rooms (9 with fireplaces)

RATES:   Single: $69 - 75,
Double: $78 - 88,
Room with a kitchenette: $88.
Credit Cards: All Major.

The Napa Valley Lodge is actually located in the interesting little town of Yountville. The surrounding land in this valley is mostly comprised of vineyards that have been operating for over a century. This two-story Spanish "hacienda" is flanked by a vineyard, a park, a grove of ancient oak trees, and gently rolling hills. The grounds are beautifully maintained with multicolored floral gardens surrounding the pool. Guests will truly appreciate the well-nurtured tranquility.

Most of the guest rooms at the lodge have a commanding view of either the pool, or the golden hills and fragrant vineyards. Subtle, simple colors such as natural beige, forest green, and navy blue make up the room decor. These various color tones are complemented by vaulted ceilings, rattan furniture, and brightly tiled bathrooms. The personal touch is also evident as your hosts provide freshly ground coffee, wine coolers and refrigerators, and live plants. Private patios or balconies are great for watching the sunset, while sipping on a glass of Napa Valley wine.

As an added note, there are special guest rooms available for $88, which have an adjoining bedroom. These are ideal for two couples or a small family. (With one group sleeping in the main room and the other enjoying the privacy of the extra bedroom.) For the complete romantic, there are also nine cozy guest chambers with fireplace.

PUPPY POLICIES: The lodge charges $5/day for your four-legged friend.

FRISKY FRIVOLITIES:
* Yountville is a quaint, wine country town, perfect for aimless wandering. If the mood is right, you may want to test yourselves on the parcourse in Yountville Park.
* Take a picnic (from the Gourmet Grape) and roam the nearby towns of St. Helena (Lyman Park), Calistoga, and Oakville.
* Show your dog your fishing prowess on the Napa River or on Lake Hennessey.

PEOPLE PLEASURES:
* Up, up, and away on a balloon or glider ride over the breathtaking hills and vineyards of Napa. Adventures Aloft is an excellent bet: (707) 255-8688.
* Learn to drive like the professionals at the Sears Point Race Track. They will teach you just how much you can expect from your car and how to make it preform in less than ideal circumstances: (707) 938-8448.
* Stop at any one of the local vineyards to sample the wine or enjoy one of their summer concerts. Domaine Chandon makes a terrific

sparkling wine and offers fine cuisine in their dining room. You may also wish to sip the fruits of their labor on the outdoor patio: (707) 944-2280.

NAPA VALLEY LODGE, Highway 29 at Madison St., Yountville, CA., 94599.

# THE VILLAGE INN
### Napa

INNKEEPERS:    Charles and Gretchen Stinnert

TELEPHONE:     (707) 257-2089

LODGING:       Eight one room cottages

RATES:         Double: $55 - 85.
               No credit cards accepted.

The Village Inn is a cozy little retreat located at the southern end of the Napa Valley. Eight newly renovated cottages are nestled in a two-acre grove of pine trees. The Stinnerts have created a perfect environment to best enjoy your Napa Valley sojourn.

Each cottage has all the modern conveniences plus a touch of country whimsy. The kitchens are fully-equipped with a dishwasher, refrigerator, and garbage disposal. French animal tiles hang on the walls and country prints adorn the windows. The couch and comforters are covered in Laura Ashley prints. In the evening, a large breakfast basket, loaded with fresh fruit and other goodies, is delivered to your door - much to the delight of either early or late risers.

The Stinnerts, who are retired teachers, are incredibly enthusiastic and helpful when it comes to planning your adventures in the area. You can also discover interesting Napa Valley "fun facts" in your private cottage library. The Stinnerts have noticed that guests who cannot finish a magazine or book during the course of their stay often take it home and try to leave a replacement. As a result, the library is in a constant state of flux, providing a unique selection of magazines and books for the next guest.

PUPPY POLICIES: Rover, Fifi, and "Odie" are a welcome addition to the Village Inn. They even have a companion, "Sasha", to play with during their vacation. The grounds are surrounded by fences to protect your dog from wandering.

FRISKY FRIVOLITIES:
   * Jog on the trail to Yountville, where you will find a parcourse (for those energetic souls).

* Go on a hike, visit the vineyards, or any of the nearby parks, and bring along a picnic. (Gourmet goodies can be found at the Oakville Grocery in Oakville.)
* Spend the day fishing at Lake Hennessey for that "one that always seems to get away".


PEOPLE PLEASURES:
* Napa and Yountville are famous for hot-air ballooning. Try Napa's Great Balloon Escape: (707) 253-0860, or Balloon Aviation: (707) 252-7067.
* Take a short trip to Calistoga where you may choose to ride on a glider, swim in a mineral pool, or relax in a mud bath.
* Test your horseback riding skills at the Wild Horse Valley in Napa.


THE VILLAGE INN, 1012 Darns Lane, Napa, CA., 94550.

# GOLD COUNTRY

Sacramento, Lake Tahoe and the Sierras

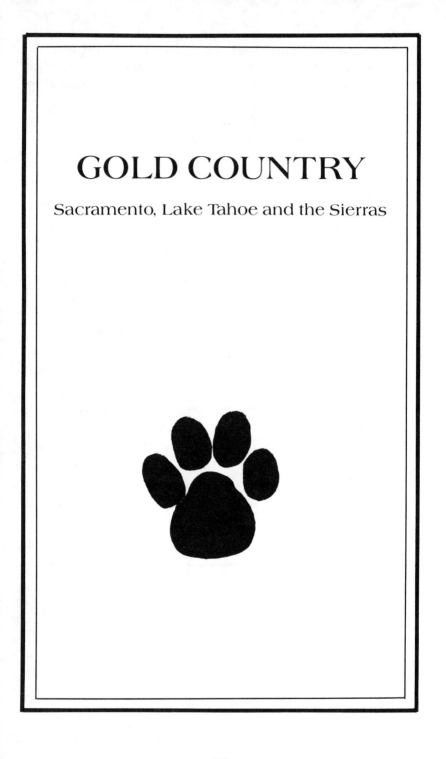

# GOLD COUNTRY

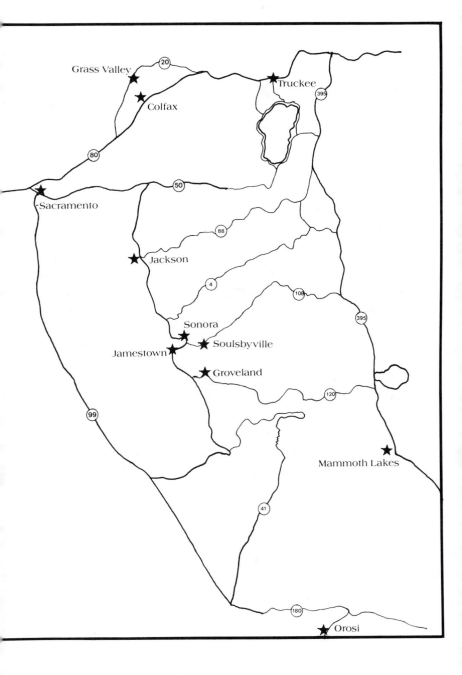

# THE BEAR FLAG INN
## Sacramento

INNKEEPER:    Robert Henry West

TELEPHONE:    (916) 448-5417

LODGING:      Two guest rooms

RATES:        Single: $40,
              Double: $50.
              Credit Cards: MC and VISA.


The Bear Flag Inn is a rambling old California house, located in a quiet residential Sacramento neighborhood. Upon stepping over the threshold, you will instantly feel at home. A cozy living room awaits you on the left, furnished with large overstuffed sofas, lovely antiques, and an elegant piano. The hardwood floors reflect the beauty of the flickering fireplace, and fresh flowers create bright areas of color throughout this spacious room.

The Willow Room is located directly off the living room. It is quite airy, with floor-to-ceiling, tie-back draperies and country antiques scattered about. The center of attention belongs to the elevated bed (a small ladder is required to get in!), and its beautifully carved headboard. An ivory lace coverlet, with subtle hints of burgandy peeking through, perfectly complements the carpet and matching patterned wallpaper. The private tiled bathroom features a ball and claw bathtub.

The Marigold Room also contains an antique bed with ornately carved headboard. A beautiful bedspread finished in a soft sand color, is adorned with forest-green throw pillows. A beveled glass mirror hangs above a simple antique chair in the corner of the room. This chamber lies toward the rear of the house and is privy to the warmth of sunlight during most of the day. The private bath is rather small and tiled in a dark green, with highlights of navy blue. There are brass fixtures for the sink and a nice stall shower to provide the finishing touches to this comfortable chamber.

You will love the special amenities your host's provide such as a well-stocked bookcase, decanter of wine, and terrific Continental breakfast. Each morning you will be greeted with a fresh cup of French roasted coffee, croissants, preserves, and grapefruit picked from the tree in the backyard. You may wish to take your breakfast on the back garden deck, and finish the morning with a gentle swing on the hammock under the shade trees.


PUPPY POLICIES: Your host gladly supplies some very comfortable accommodations in his enclosed backyard for your traveling pal ($10 per night).


FRISKY FRIVOLITIES:
* If you are looking for an enervating workout, try the El Rancho Parcourse Jogging Trail that winds over more than 17 acres. (NOTE: Sacramento has a strict leash law.)
* The residential neighborhoods on the way to Capitol Park are filled with Victorian relics. Walk the route to the park and continue on to the Old Governor's Mansion (home of thirteen governors) located on 16th and H.
* Enjoy a pleasant day-trip to Auburn State Park: (916) 885-4527, overlooking the Auburn

Dam and old mining caves (which date back to 1850). An alternate excursion might include fishing on the American River, or watching fish growth cycles at the nearby Nimbus Fish Hatcheries: (916) 445-3531.

PEOPLE PLEASURES:
* The inn is located only five minutes from the State Capitol, built in 1861. It has recently been restored and you may take hourly tours.
* Sutter's Fort is two blocks away and although it was built in 1839, it is still in terrific condition. John Sutter originally built this Swiss settlement and called it "New Helveta".
* Another type of cultural exhibit that you may wish to delve into, is the contemporary art collection which is featured at the Crocker Art Museum: (916) 446-4677, or the Artist's Collaborative Gallery: (916) 444-3764.

THE BEAR FLAG INN, 2814 I Street, Sacramento, CA., 95816.

---

# SWAN-LEVINE HOUSE
## Grass Valley

INNKEEPERS: Peggy and Howard Levine

TELEPHONE: (916) 272-1873

LODGING: Six rooms

RATES: Room: $35 - 50.
No credit cards accepted.

The Swan-Levine House was originally built in the late 1870's, as a private family residence. Dr. John Jones and his brothers then purchased this old Victorian in 1895 and converted it into a small hospital. In the years that followed, the hospital was transformed into a community medical center. Peggy Swan and Howard Levine bought the soon to be bed & breakfast in 1975 and began the ten year refurbishing process, which continues to this day.

Their first order of business was to restore the decaying structure to its original charm. As you head up the walkway, the newly built pool sits invitingly off to the left and fragrant magnolia and apple trees line the right-hand side of the yard. Directly ahead lies the gigantic porch of the inn, exhibiting some of the more recent effort behind this restoration project.

Once inside, you will find hardwood floors stretching throughout the house. Your eyes will wander to the many tiled fireplaces that seem to inhabit every corner. The overall character of the inn is suggested in an interesting juxtaposition of antiques with Peggy and Howard's progressive art pieces. While in the parlor, you should take note of Peggy's great-great-grandmother's intricately handwoven paisley shawl that hangs on a wall next to the Levine's juke box. The eclectic combination of art and innkeeping is the precise reason these two opted to go into business. They even have a studio in the backyard specifically for artists and visiting novices, who want to practice a little lithography (both stone and plate), etching, and engraving. Of course, you may also come to the Swan-Levine House to simply savor a truly unique bed and breakfast experience.

Their artistic flair is in evidence throughout the house. On the second floor you will find pieces ranging from pastels and pen-and-ink drawings to computer graphics and pottery. The corridors also house special surprises, larger-than-lifesize, brightly painted standup cardboard figures. Each guest room has also benefitted from the Levine's artistic touch. The quilts draped over the beds were handmade by Peggy. The colors also vary according to the room decor, which ranges from electric pink or vibrant green combinations to deep blue and purple.

Antiques are abundant in each of the five spacious guest chambers. Our favorite was the suite with private bath and cozy sitting room (with a library and wood burning fireplace). Across the hallway is the original operating room, with a set of enormous windows providing a terrific view of the flowering magnolia. If you are traveling with the "wee ones", your hosts have the perfect room with two bunk beds. The two remaining rooms are further down the hall. One is painted in a bright royal blue, and the other, a deep forest green with a contrasting upper white wall. The latter few bedrooms contain their own wash basins, and share a gigantic bathroom with a large ball and claw foot tub.

Breakfast is orchestrated by Howard and will vary, depending upon his creative mood and "what happens to be in the house at the time".


PUPPY POLICIES: Peggy and Howard eagerly look forward to your visit. They do ask that you do not leave your furry friend unattended.


FRISKY FRIVOLITIES:
  * Walking tours of Nevada City: (916) 265-2692 and Grass Valley: (916) 273-5939 are both interesting and invigorating.

* Terrific hiking and cross-country skiing trails are found throughout the Emigrant Gap and Lake Tahoe areas (ask Howard for details).
* You will find excellent canoeing and fishing opportunities on either the American, Yuba, or Bear rivers.


PEOPLE PLEASURES:
* A step into the past is possible with a visit to Empire Park, composed of elegant gardens and one of California's oldest gold mines (it yielded 5,800,000 ounces of gold until 1956): (916) 273-8522.
* Test out the terrific Alpine skiing at Alpine Meadows, Squaw Valley or Borreal Ridge.
* The American Victorian Museum exhibits an 1878 Pelton wheel, antique Steinway pianos, and Victorian toys and games: (916) 273-9853.


SWAN-LEVINE HOUSE, 328 South Church Street, Grass Valley, CA., 95945.

---

# BEAR RIVER MOUNTAIN FARM
## Colfax


INNKEEPER:     Lynne Lewis

TELEPHONE:     (916) 878-8314

LODGING:       Three bedrooms

RATES:         Rooms: $40 - 50.
               No credit cards accepted.

The Bear River Mountain Farm is located on three lush acres in the midst of the Gold Country. The farmhouse is a cute little cottage surrounded by maple, magnolia, and willow trees. The beauty and ambiance of this natural setting is further enhanced by the beehives that produce delicious manzanita and blackberry honey. Cool climates, thick foliage, and friendly hospitality help to set this tranquil scene. Occasionally, the calm is broken by the grey herons, turtles, ducks, and other little creatures bickering and scurrying about the pond.

The farmhouse is just a short distance from Lynne's house. Guests will enjoy the opportunity to explore this scenic area or just relax on the wood trestle porch, while the world passes by. The B&B quarters feature two bedrooms upstairs, with a pair of twin beds and one queen bed. In the downstairs room, a king-sized bed awaits the true "bed hog". The frills, or lack of them, are based upon your desire to "rough it". Guests may either choose to bring their own linens or opt for the bed and breakfast plan, which includes linens, firewood, and a hearty breakfast. In either case, you will enjoy the use of modern amenities such as a stereo, television, fully-equipped kitchen, and living room.

PUPPY POLICIES: Lynne Lewis gladly welcomes your canine cohort with plenty of advance notice. She also asks for a non-refundable $15/cleaning fee.

FRISKY FRIVOLITIES:
* There are miles of local hiking trails and exciting areas to explore along Bear River.

* Cross-country skiing is a seasonal pastime in these parts, and many dogs enjoy bounding through the snowy fields and woods.
* Visit Rollins Lake for a little fishing, boating, or picnicking.

PEOPLE PLEASURES:
* Drive south of Colfax through Placerville and down to Jackson. Along the way you might want to you stop in Amador City and Sutter Creek for shopping and sightseeing.
* The American River is an excellent spot to enjoy wild river rafting or tubing.
* Grass Valley, North Bloomfield, and Nevada City are only a short drive from the farm. Along the way you will see old mining towns, the discovery site of an 18 lb. gold nugget, Malakoff Diggings, American Museum, Bourn Mansion, and many other interesting places.

BEAR RIVER MOUNTAIN FARM, 21725 Placer Hills Road, Colfax, CA., 95713.

---

# BRADLEY HOUSE
## Truckee

INNKEEPERS:    Donna and Larry Bradley

TELEPHONE:     (916) 587-5388

LODGING:       6 rooms, shared baths

RATES:         Double: $40 - 60.
               No credit cards accepted.

The Bradley House overlooks the heart of old Truckee, a lumber town that is currently in the midst of a substantial revitalization. This 1880 Victorian home was once owned by a lumber baron and is at present being lovingly restored to its original charm by the Bradleys. Several features of special interest are the original wainscoting up the staircase wall, the intricate pine woodworking, and the hand carved picket fence which surrounds the property.

The five upstairs bedrooms are decorated in browns, blues, and whites. The high beds are adorned with Amish quilts and have either massive pine or iron bedsteads. There is an eclectic selection of comfortable antique furniture in all of the rooms, along with a terrific assortment of 1950's memorabilia (advertisements, magazines, and pictures). All of these amenities add to the overall "home-away-from-home" atmosphere. These cozy accommodations do not contain private baths, thus you will share with your neighbor. The bathrooms are nicely divided though, with a large separate shower/bath and water closet in one room and another W.C. and double sink in the other.

Downstairs, in The Cabin room, there is a television, wood stove, private bathroom, and a separate entrance. It is a bit more rustic than the other accommodations, but does offer privacy.

In the morning, a generous Continental breakfast of fresh fruit, muffins, and scrumptious apple strudel greet those with hearty appetites. Each afternoon between 5 p.m. and 6 p.m., your hosts present an appetizing selection of cheese and wine to their guests.

PUPPY POLICIES: The Bradleys welcome your dog provided you notify them in advance and do not leave him/her alone in the room. Your hosts have several cats and would greatly appreciate it if your dog's "cat manners" were exemplary.

FRISKY FRIVOLITIES:
* There are terrific cross-country ski trails in the area for Nordic fun. During the summer months there are wide-open fields for you to explore. Investigate the endless hiking trails throughout the North Lake Tahoe region.
* D.L Bliss State Park lies between Meeks and Emerald Bay. Over 1,200 acres lie waiting to be explored. There is also a terrific sandy beach near Rubicon Point.
* This region is "dog country" and short trips through Truckee, Tahoe City, and Incline will give you a chance to explore and shop, while your dog makes a few new friends.

PEOPLE PLEASURES:
- * Ski some of the best snow conditions in the country at Squaw Valley, Incline Village, and Alpine Meadows.
- * During the warmer months, Lake Tahoe is an excellent area for windsurfing, sailing, and boating (there are motor boat races in the late summer).
- * For those who feel "money is no object", a gambling trip to South Lake Tahoe or Reno is an exciting way to spend a day (and your $).

THE BRADLEY HOUSE, P.O. Box 2011, Truckee, CA., 95734.

---

# COURT STREET INN
## Jackson

INNKEEPER:  Mildred Burns

TELEPHONE:  (209) 223-0416

LODGING:  Six Rooms

RATES:  Rooms:  $60 - 105
Low season and weekday rates available.
No credit cards accepted.

The Court Street Inn was originally built by Edward Muldoon, for the Peisers, in 1872. Then, around the turn-of-the-century, the Blair family added a second story to the house and used it as a Wells Fargo office. Several decades later, Grace Depue, the Blair's daughter, inherited the house from her parents. From this time until her death, Grace amassed an impressive collection of Indian artifacts, which she displayed in a small house in the backyard.

Mildred Burns is the present day owner and innkeeper of the Court Street Inn. She happened upon the property some years ago during one of her many visits to the area. This time she found the "niche" she had been searching for and bought the building. In May of 1980 she started the long restoration process, soon realizing that a potential inner beauty and charm truly did exist in this Gold Country relic. After stripping the linoleum off of the natural hardwood floors, scraping layers of paint from the walls, and dressing up a tattered brick fireplace with a new marble front, the inn was beginning to show signs of life. Today, the Court Street Inn glows, and upon entering the house you will immediately recognize that this is truly a special place.

There are six bedrooms available to guests.

One of the more noteworthy chambers is the Peiser Room, with a private sun porch. Decorated with a combination of very impressive antiques and rattan furniture, this green and white room has a certain vibrancy to it. You will want to look carefully for Mildred's special touches, such as the classic baby buggy and photographs, set off by vases of fresh flowers. The handmade quilt definitely puts the finishing touches on this room.

Yet another guest room is located across from a beautiful redwood deck. This is actually an old work shed that has been painstakingly converted into an elegantly appointed bedroom. A ceiling fan cools the cozy sitting area; while the airy skylight sheds sun onto the queen bed resting on top of its raised platform. Each bedroom is as charming as the next. Most are adorned with delicate wallpaper set off by handmade quilts, potted flowers and plants.

The common rooms of the house also hold fine collectibles. French doors will lead you into the dining room. Oriental rugs, dozens of figurines, and an ebony lacquered Chinese screen surround you. Take time, during afternoon tea or wine to ask Mildred a few questions about these treasures.

Each morning Mildred serves a full-breakfast of delectables, such as homemade bread, quiche, crepes, fresh berries, and coffee or tea. After enjoying this fabulous meal, superb hospitality, and accommodations, you will look forward to a return visit.


PUPPY POLICIES: Your dog is a welcome addition to the Court Street Inn if it is small and if you plan a weekday visit. Mildred will not be able to accommodate your dog during busy weekends.

## FRISKY FRIVOLITIES:

* Try your hand at the local fishing, an ideal way to spend the afternoon. Bob Leslie's Fishing Guide Service: (209) 532-4453 offers experienced guides.
* Bring your dog to Indian Grinding Rock State Park to see, among other things, a 7,700 square foot rock covered with 1,200 mortar holes make by the Miwok Indians. This is the only park dedicated to the Indian culture.
* From Jackson continue down the road toward the other historic gold mine towns. Angel's Camp, Murphys, Volcano, and Sonora are well worth a visit.


## PEOPLE PLEASURES:

* Raft the wild rapids on the many nearby rivers with O.A.R.S. River Trips: (209) 736-4677.
* Visit the State Capitol and explore the many interesting sites in the city. Take a walking tour through Old Sacramento: (916) 443-7815, visit the Railroad Museum: (916) 372-3690, or just enjoy the inviting shopping.
* Spend the day exploring the Delta with "Delta & Bay Cruises": (916) 372-3690.


COURT STREET INN, 215 Court Street, Jackson, CA., 95642.

# GUNN HOUSE
## Sonora

INNKEEPER:      Peggy Schoell

TELEPHONE:      (209) 532-3421

LODGING:        25 rooms

RATES:          Double: $37.80 - 61.56.
                Credit Cards: AE, MC, and VISA.


    The Gunn House is centrally located on the main street of Sonora, creating a perfect base for visitors to the "Mother Lode". This house, as an historical landmark, has an very interesting story behind it, and a good deal of tender loving care has gone into its restoration. Dr. Lewis C. Gunn, the Mother Lode's first newspaper editor, built the house during a controversial newspaper episode in 1890.

    In the mid 1960's, Margaret Dienelt purchased the Gunn House and started collecting all of the antiques she could locate in the surrounding towns and villages. Now, after three generations of construction and refurbishing, the rooms display an eclectic mix of modern amenities and antique furnishings. A few of the special features are wrought-iron bedsteads covered in hand-quilted bedspreads, carved wood chairs, marble-topped tables, and many unique paintings. You will also appreciate the modern conveniences, such as color television, air-conditioning, and a private bath.

    Guests will probably spend a portion of their sojourn relaxing around the pool or surrounded by flowers on one of the covered verandas. Perhaps a visit to the Josephine Room is just what you need. By night it is a popular bar, while each morning it is the site of an ample Continental breakfast.


PUPPY POLICIES: Your dog is a welcome addition to the Gunn House for a $4/night fee. Please make advance reservations for your cohort.


FRISKY FRIVOLITIES:
* Taste some of nature's finest during visits to Sonka's Apple Ranch: (209) 928-4689, the Stevenot: (209) 728-3436, and the Stoneridge Vineyard: (209) 223-1761.
* Your dog will enjoy a side trip to Yosemite National Park (dogs must be leashed). You may wish to rise early to spend the entire day basking in this magnificent valley's splendor.
* Jog or walk with your dog down any of the country roads surrounding Sonora. A short drive out of town toward the Sierra foothills will bring you to miles of untouched hills and valleys.


PEOPLE PLEASURES:
* Take a journey back into time during a visit to the prehistoric Moaning Cavern in nearby Vallecito: (209) 736-2708.
* A tour of the Gold Country is not complete without visiting the historic Sutter Creek. The town has been meticulously restored over the years, and is reminiscent of a quaint New England village.

* Recreate Mother Lode gold rush days with visits to the old west towns of Columbia, China Camp, and Jamestown.

GUNN HOUSE, 286 South Washington, Sonora, CA., 95370.

---

# THE RYAN HOUSE
## Sonora

INNKEEPER:    Maureen Kelley

TELEPHONE:    (209) 533-3445

LODGING:      Four guest rooms

RATES:        Rooms: $45 - 55
              Credit Cards:  MC and VISA.

The Ryan House bed and breakfast is tucked away on a quiet street in Sonora. This charming little house was originally built for Dennis and Susan Ryan in the 1850's, and over the course of a century it expanded to meet the needs of their growing family. Time took a toll on the structure, and when Maureen Kelley purchased it in 1983, she realized she was faced with a major restoration project.

Since then, her masterful hand has renewed the home, and her green thumb has brightened the gardens. Everywhere you look there are well-kept lawns, vibrant groupings of spring flowers and shade trees. Once inside the house you will find that Maureen has been hard at work redecorating the bedrooms. She has turned this B&B into what is truly a "home-away-from-home".

Each of the rooms is handsomely appointed with country antiques, hand-carved headboards, and cotton bedspreads (handmade quilts lie at the end of the beds). The Garden Room is painted a soft baby blue, with plants of all shapes and sizes adorning the tables and window sills. This is the most appropriate room for you and your dog, since it is fashioned with a private entrance leading out onto the garden.

The Lavender Room and Mae's Room (cleverly named after Mae Ryan, the last Ryan to inhabit it) flank the Garden Room. If you love rose tones, the former is the spot for you while Mae's Room is a nice, big, corner room painted in a pale blue. These three rooms share a large, full-bath with a stall shower. The Lavender Room is the exception as it does have a half-bath. Painted in a pastel yellow, the Sun Room is privy to sunshine most of the day. Maureen's grandmother's multi-colored, wedding ring quilt adorns the bed, and serves to further brighten the chamber. Best of all, this room also contains a cozy, private bath.

You will be interested to learn that there is no central heating in the house, but the deluxe wood burning stove in the living room easily warms all of the rooms. Here you might encounter one of the house cats, who also enjoy the warmth of the fire. Each room has an individually controlled heater that will keep you toasty warm all through the night.

Each morning you will awaken to wondrous smells from the kitchen signaling a scrumptious breakfast is in the works. You may want to enjoy this culinary delight in the dining room, on the porch, or in the yard under the gently swaying hawthorne tree.

PUPPY POLICIES: Maureen will gladly accept your small canine companion. She does ask that he/she is well-behaved and has "cat manners".

FRISKY FRIVOLITIES:
* Sonora is in the heart of the Gold Country. Many of the nearby towns are much the same as they were 100 years ago and are great fun to explore.
* For those who would like to "get back to nature", there are superb hiking trails in Calaveras Big Trees State Park.
* Visit the Tuolumne River and enjoy a picnic, or some wild, river rafting.

PEOPLE PLEASURES:
* Maureen offers winter guests package deals that include either downhill or cross-country skiing at some of the nearby resorts (starting at $30/person).

* A trip to Jamestown will bring you to the Railtown 1897 roundhouse, which displays old train engines. Here you may wish to take a ride on the Sierra Railroad.
* Columbia State Park is a preserved Gold Rush town which recalls the rough and tumble days of the 1850's. Enjoy riding an authentic stagecoach or visiting the blacksmith, old-time saloon, wild west museum, and/or the Fallon House Theater (which still presents plays). The hard rock mine is a good place to learn how to pan for gold.

RYAN HOUSE, P.O. Box 416, 153 S. Shepherd St., Sonora, CA., 95370.

---

# WILLOW SPRINGS COUNTRY INN
### Soulsbyville

INNKEEPERS: Karen and Marty Wheeler

TELEPHONE: (209) 533-2030

LODGING: Five rooms with double or
queen beds

RATES: Double: $50 and up.
No credit cards accepted.


This rambling house was originally built by
Ben Soulsbyville, the very wealthy prospector who
founded the town. It is ideally located in the
midst of surrounding hills and carefully tended
lawns and gardens. The principle porch that once
encircled the house now has several functions
which include use as the entry way, a kitchen,
and a living room (filled with comfortable wicker
furnishings). Once guests venture inside, they
will find that many of the original rooms (ie: the
kitchen and living room) have been transformed
into truly unique guest bedrooms.
Each is nicely furnished with an overhead
fan, soft, ruffled bed sheets and pillow cases, and
vases overflowing with fresh flowers. The frills of
day-to-day life, such as televisions, private baths
and telephones are not featured at this quaint inn.
This might be a welcome exclusion for those who
wish "to get away from it all" and experience the
simple elegance and quiet charm of the inn.
Each morning begins with a complimentary
breakfast on the porch, featuring fresh fruit and
rolls or bread. On the weekends, a much heartier
breakfast is served with a fine selection of crepes,
quiche, fruit, and several types of fresh pastries.
Afterward, you may want to take advantage of the
adjoining recreational facilities. A refreshing dip

in the lake, a set of tennis, or a horseshoe pitch, are the ways most guests like to spend the quieter hours of the day. Whether you spend your free time enjoying the inn's activities or exploring the historic surrounding areas, everyone is cordially invited back to the inn for an afternoon of wine, hors d'oeuvres, and engaging conversation.

PUPPY POLICIES: The Wheelers will gladly welcome your little friend provided you give them enough advance notice.

FRISKY FRIVOLITIES:
* The grounds around the inn are perfect for wandering with curious canines.
* You may want to spend your day panning for a few nuggets of gold in several of the local rivers. Bring your old "sniffer" as he/she may help to increase your odds of finding your fortune: (209) 533-2670.
* The Calaveras Big Trees are a dog's "dream come true" - seriously though, this park houses fine examples of the giant sequoias.

PEOPLE PLEASURES:
* Run the wild waters on one of California's finest rivers with O.A.R.S.: (209) 736-4677 or (209) 736-2924.
* Take a step back in time and spend the day at the Columbia State Historical Park where visitors can ride 100 year old stages, sample old west cooking, visit the museums, or watch craftsmen demonstrating their wares.
* Ride a turn-of-the-century train and see many others still in operable condition at the historic Railtown: (209) 984-3953.

WILLOW SPRINGS COUNTRY INN, 20599 Kings Ct., Soulsbyville, CA., 95372.

# THE NATIONAL HOTEL
## Jamestown

INNKEEPER:   Stephen Willey

TELEPHONE:   (209) 984-3446

LODGING:   11 bedrooms

RATES:   Double w/private bath:  $45,
Double w/shared bath:  $35.
Credit Cards:  AE, MC, and VISA.


The historic National Hotel was built in 1859 and catered to overnight guests until ravaged by fire in the 1920's. The rebuilt hotel was ultimately purchased by the Willey family in 1974, but neglect had taken its toll on the foundation, wiring, and plumbing, and it soon became apparent to Stephen Willey he had a monumental restoration task before him. Working with limited funds, and doing most of the carpentry himself, Stephen has carefully brought much of the hotel back to its original splendor. Even more recently, work on the front porch and the facade have been completed and now truly reflect their 18th century heritage.

The 11 bedrooms are the most recent project. Their decor is simple; brass beds covered with patchwork quilts, period wallpaper, and antique furniture. Room furnishings are in constant flux because Stephen is always making new additions. All of the rooms have antique wash basins, and you can opt for either a private or shared bath. Whichever your decision, you will enjoy the pull chain toilets and stall showers. For those who still relish the modern amenities, all rooms have air-conditioning and electric heating. By the way, televisions may be requested.

Downstairs, visitors will marvel at the antique cash register and the massive redwood bar in the saloon. The dining room is still in the process of being restored, although this has not hampered its reputation as "one of the finest (restaurants) in the Mother Lode". Each morning you can enjoy a Continental breakfast in either the dining room or, weather permitting, the Garden Courtyard.

PUPPY POLICIES: The Willeys eagerly welcome your canine companion provided he/she is well behaved and of the lap variety.

FRISKY FRIVOLITIES:
* Let your dog step back in history and take him/her for a walk along the raised wooden sidewalks, by the picturesque old buildings to the Jamestown Railway Depot.
* The drive to Yosemite is magnificent! You will truly enjoy investigating the valley floor, picnicking along the river's edge, and taking advantage of this renowned, awe-inspiring spot. (Dogs must be leashed in the park.)
* If your dog prefers a day in the water, then hike along the banks of the Tuolumne River. You may want to fish for trout, while your furry friend romps along the shore.

PEOPLE PLEASURES
* If you are a railroad aficionado, choose from a variety of excursions on an old steam train. The Railtown 1897 State Historic Park offers a variety of tours through the Sierra canyons and foothills: (209) 984-3935.

* Take the walking tour of Sonora consisting of 20 historic buildings. The walking guide-map can be found at the Chamber of Commerce.
* Believe it or not, Calaveras County actually has a frog jumping contest. It is held each year in Angel's Camp.

NATIONAL HOTEL, Main Street, P.O. Box 502, Jamestown, CA., 95327.

---

# HOTEL CHARLOTTE
## Groveland

INNKEEPERS:  Jim and Ruth Kraenzel

TELEPHONE:    (209) 962-6455

LODGING:      14 rooms/suites

RATES:        Single:  $35 - 45,
                  Double:  $45 - 55,
                  2 Bedroom Suite:  $85 - 90.
                  Credit Cards:  MC and VISA.

The Hotel Charlotte lies at the gateway to Yosemite Valley, making it a natural overnight refuge for people going to, or coming from, this valley. It is also perfectly situated for those who want to make it a base camp for their expeditions throughout the rest of this spectacular region.

This historical building is situated in the heart of Groveland. The weathered sign in front of the hotel announces that "Rooms, Zimmers, or Pensions" are available inside. Upon entering the hotel, you will find a cozy lobby, decorated with simple country furniture. There is also a dining room, to the left of the lobby, boasting a hearty fare of fine home cooking.

A forest-green carpeted stairway leads guests to their bedrooms. These chambers run the length of a long hallway, and are generally the same size. They are furnished with country American antique dressers, bedside tables, and painted wrought-iron bedsteads. You may select from either double or queen beds, and private or shared baths. If you decide to share a bath, comical wallpaper of various sudsy cartoon characters will amuse you while relaxing in the ball and claw foot tub. Also located at the end of the hallway is a common room with a television and comfortable couches.

For those who are visiting for several days, we highly recommend inquiring about the hotel's Cross-Country Skiing, River Rafting, Golfing, or Gold Panning packages. These offer you terrific bargains, ranging from $65 to $310.

PUPPY POLICIES: The Kraenzels will welcome your mountain-bound dog, provided he/she is very well-behaved.


FRISKY FRIVOLITIES:
* Visit Tuolumne Meadows, located in the heart of the High Sierra (8,592 Ft.), where you will have the opportunity to fish and hike by the mountain streams.
* A short trip to nearby Coulterville will give visitors the chance to explore a revitalized old mining town. Lake McClure offers a wide assortment of recreational activities including, swimming, sailing, fishing, and picnicking.
* Wawona Basin is a terrific recreation area in Yosemite Valley, offering picnic sites and hiking through the scenic meadows.


PEOPLE PLEASURES:
* Take a trip back to the old Gold Rush days during visits to the historic towns of Angels Camp, Murphys, Columbia, and Jamestown.
* Test your Alpine skiing prowess on Badger Pass or cross-country ski through Yosemite Park.
* The beauty of this area lies in the outdoors. Now that you have left civilization behind, you are free to explore the wilds of this protected park.


HOTEL CHARLOTTE, Highway 120, P.O. Box 884, Groveland, CA., 95321.

# SNOW GOOSE INN
## Mammoth Lakes

INNKEEPER:   Andrew Solt

TELEPHONE:   (619) 934-2660

LODGING:   16 guest rooms, 4 suites

RATES:   Guest Room: $50 - 60,
Room with Kitchenette: $60 - 70,
Deluxe Suite: $90 - 100.
Credit Cards: MC and VISA.

The Snow Goose Inn is just a short stroll from downtown Mammoth. This New England-style inn, painted in a soft grey-blue, has offered guests a wide variety of cozy accommodations ever since 1980.

All of the rooms are simply, but comfortably furnished. The wicker, brass, or oak bedsteads provide lovely backdrops to the comfortable beds covered with floral bedspreads. (Mints are placed on your pillow in the evening). Spacious private bathrooms contain a shower/bath, double sinks set in a marble-like base, and most importantly, all cotton towels.

The inn also has four suites located in a separate building offering similar amenities, yet more space. Most have two guest bedrooms on the first floor, while upstairs you will find a fully-stocked kitchen, separate dining area, and living room with a fireplace. The carpeting is either a deep green or brown, and is complemented with a delicate French country flower-print wallpaper. An assortment of knick-knacks abound, for example, in one of the living rooms there is an old wooden clock hanging on the wall that is over three feet in circumference.

After unpacking and relaxing, you may wish to migrate to the living room, which is decorated in a country blue-and-white checked wallpaper set off beautifully by the dark wood-beamed ceilings. The walls are filled with a dozen or so oversized posters of paintings by Cezanne, Picasso, Van Gough, and other European masters. You will be amazed by the numbers of stuffed toys, ceramic figurines, and paintings of geese in the living room. (You don't have to be an avid goose fan to enjoy these little critters!) This motif is further enhanced by the wide assortment of brass lamps and candle holders, several comfortably-stuffed sofas, American country antiques, and the subtly placed large-screen television.

PUPPY POLICIES: Andrew also has a dog who is always eager to meet another canine companion. Andrew asks that you not leave yours unattended in the room.

FRISKY FRIVOLITIES:
* For those dogs who enjoy the outdoors, there are schools of brook, rainbow, and enormous brown trout waiting to be chased or caught in the local lakes.
* Hike up Mammoth Mountain - this can be a bit strenuous, but always provides breathtaking views of the surrounding valleys and ridges (especially of the Minarets).
* Visit the Bodie State Historical Park (17 miles north of Lee Vining). This is a deserted old gold mine town (of the late 1800's). Many of

the original buildings still contain the tools and provisions of the Bodie miners.

PEOPLE PLEASURES:
* A perfect way to end the day is with a sports or Swedish massage available at Body Focus Massage: (619) 934-4001.
* The Hot Creek Fish Hatchery (8a.m. - 5p.m.) illustrates the developmental stages of trout from spawning to maturity.
* A picnic at Rainbow Falls (1 mile from Reds Meadow) is an ideal way to enjoy lunch or the remainder of the afternoon. These falls are created by the San Joaquin River plunging over a lava edge into a deep gorge 140 feet below.

SNOW GOOSE INN, P.O. Box 946, Mammoth Lakes, CA., 93546.

# TAMARACK LODGE RESORT
## Mammoth Lakes

INNKEEPERS:  Asher Family

TELEPHONE:  (619) 934-2442

LODGING:  30 housekeeping cabins

RATES:  Cabin: $40 - 124.
Credit Cards:  All Major


    The Tamarack Lodge was originally built in 1924 to provide lodging for hunters and fishermen during their mountain treks. More recently, it has been transformed into a year-round resort, catering to skiers and hikers. One of the many outstanding features of this historic lodge is its ideal location, in the heart of the Sierra Nevada mountains, on the shores of Twin Lakes.

    You will enjoy the wide selection of guest cabins. Each offers "something special", and you may choose the one that most appropriately meets your needs. Set on the perimeter of the Twin Lakes, the cabins adhere to the rustic decor of the main lodge (constructed during the 1920's and 30's). The kitchens are fully-equipped, and a few of the spacious living rooms have wood burning stoves or fireplaces. Fisherman's Cabin and Cabin Number 3 are the largest, sleeping up to 10 or 12 people, respectively.

    Once you are settled, do visit the main lodge with its rustically furnished living room and huge stone fireplace. While you are out and about, you might wish to sample the delicious fare at the Lakefront Restaurant. Their selections of entrees range from "Black Forest" lamb and quail, to fresh seafood. An excellent way to top off the evening is with a delicious assortment of pastries and desserts. While relaxing over a cup of coffee, you

101

will enjoy the scenic views of the lake, waterfalls, and distant mountains through the picture window.

To fully work off any remnants of a lingering dinner or overly satiating breakfast, the lodge offers a plethora of cross-country ski trails for beginners and experts. For those who feel a little bit more adventuresome, there are many ski bowls and scenic mountain trails around Mammoth.

PUPPY POLICIES: The lodge gladly welcomes your furry friend (cabin rooms only).

FRISKY FRIVOLITIES:
* Visit one of the many local lakes: Horseshoe (great swimming), Mamie (hikes over pass to Mcleod Lake, Red Cones), and Lake George (trails up to Red's Meadow).
* The Inyo Craters are the three remnants of a volcanic blast which took place over 100 years ago (this is a great spot for sightseeing and picnicking).
* "Outdoor dogs" will love a swim in the Twin Lakes while "city-dogs" may prefer a walk through Mammoth Village.

PEOPLE PLEASURES:
* Snowmobile rentals and tours are available on the Smokey Bear Flats: (619) 935-4480.
* Visit Devil's Postpile - a highly unusual rock formation resulting from lava pouring through Mammoth Pass. Once the earth and molten rock finally cooled, there were 3 to 7 sided columns ranging from 40 to 60 feet high.
* Mammoth offers some of the very best Alpine and cross-country skiing in California.

TAMARACK LODGE RESORT, P.O. Box 69, Mammoth Lakes, CA., 93546.

# VALLEY VIEW CITRUS RANCH
### Orosi

INNKEEPERS: Ruth and Tom Flippen

TELEPHONE: (209) 528-2275

LODGING: 3 guest rooms

RATES: Single: $42,
Double: $45.
No credit cards accepted.

The Valley View Citrus Ranch is located in San Joaquin Valley, at the base of the Sierra Nevada foothills. This valley, known at the "fruit basket of the nation" is planted with everything from almonds and avocados to tangelos and grapes. You will find, with the change of seasons, either fragrant and colorful blossoms, or trees and fields heavily laden with ripe fruits and vegetables.

This Spanish-style ranch, built in 1964, is covered with vines of flowering bougainvillaea. These line the 70 foot porch where guests often spend the afternoons talking over a glass of wine or fresh orange juice. These "sessions" often last into the evening as people love to watch the sun set over the Sierra foothills. If the night turns cool then the wood-paneled living room is waiting, complete with a roaring fire.

The two bedrooms are located in the main house, off of the living room. These twin-bedded accommodations are very simply furnished, with comfortably overstuffed furniture and wall-to-wall carpeting. Both rooms have Spanish-tiled wash basins and share a bath down the hall. If you prefer more solitude or a private bath, then the

103

Indian Room is for you. Set away from the main house, this cottage has spectacular views of the surrounding hills. Do take some time to look at the interesting collection of Indian wall hangings. If the night becomes too warm, you can just turn on your air-conditioning. (All of the rooms have an "AC" unit.)

Each morning a full breakfast is served to guests on the porch or under the gazebo. You may also request picnic lunches for afternoon strolls among the wild flowers. While away the afternoon with a tennis match on the clay court or a game of volleyball. There are also horseshoes and board games if you prefer less strenuous activities.


PUPPY POLICIES: The Flippens welcome your furry friend with advance notice.


FRISKY FRIVOLITIES:
* This valley is perfect for long walks in the surrounding foothills. Depending upon the time of year, you could see wild flowers, the golden summer grasses, or a myriad of colors announcing the start of fall.
* Visit the Sequoia and Kings Canyon National Parks just east of the inn. There are over 1,300 acres to hike on, streams to fish in, and in the winter, cross-country skiing.
* Mineral King is a picturesque and secluded valley set below towering Sierra mountain peaks. It offers visitors a scenic peek into an unspoiled land. There are also terrific streams for trout fishing!

## PEOPLE PLEASURES:

* Explore Boyden Caverns which offer a variety of underground formations: (209) 736-2708.
* Sun-Maid Raisin has the largest packing plant in the world, just a few minutes from the ranch. Their tour is most informative.
* There are several golf courses in the area, offering a variety of challenges. Your hosts will be able to suggest an appropriate one for you.

THE VALLEY VIEW CITRUS RANCH, 14801 Ave. 428, Orosi, CA., 93647.

# BAY AREA

San Francisco, Marin, and the East Bay

# BAY AREA

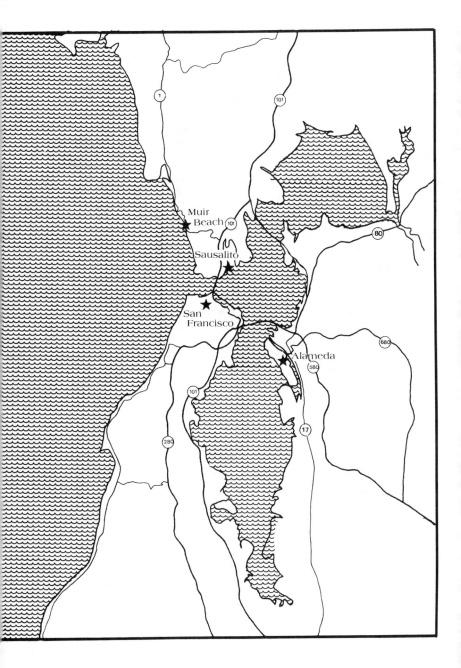

# THE PELICAN INN
## Muir Beach

INNKEEPER:      Barry Scott

TELEPHONE:      (415) 383-6000

LODGING:        6 cozy English rooms

RATES:          Double:  $90.
                Credit Cards:  MC and VISA.


    The Pelican Inn derives its name from Sir Francis Drake's vessel, which beached itself upon this Marin coast some 400 years ago.  This is truly an inn for those romantic souls, as it captures the atmosphere and spirit of a 16th century English hostelry.

    Each of the six rooms has a raised canopied bed, English antiques, and Oriental rugs covering dark pegged-wood floors.  The guest chambers are cozy, but just in case they become chilly, a small bottle of sherry is left by your bed to warm you.

If you look at the ceiling you will notice a stone with a hole in it hung over your bed; this is to ensure "no rickets in case of pregnancy". You may also see pennies stuck in the cracks of the wood-beams; these will bring good luck.

After a peaceful night of sleep, you will awaken to a full English breakfast (served in your room). If you are not a "breakfast person" then please try the delicious dinners at the inn. Their menu is strictly English country-style and includes favorites such as bangers, meat pies, homemade breads, fresh salads (and a few local specialties). Depending upon the season, you may wish to take your meal on either the terrace or in front of the roaring five foot fireplace. If you are celebrating a special occasion, then you may want to request an authentic Elizabethan feast. This features a few minstrels, wenches, mead or wine, and a wild assortment of roasted English delicacies.

The inn also has an authentic English pub to help you while away the hours with many of the local crowd. Choose from their wide assortment of beer, port, and wine. You may also play darts or just marvel at their collection of paper money from all over the world stuck to the ceiling.


PUPPY POLICIES: They welcome the four-legged variety without damage deposit or nightly charge.


FRISKY FRIVOLITIES:
   * Muir Beach is a 2-3 minute stroll from the inn. You will find a nice sandy beach to play on and great rock formations to climb.
   * There are ample hiking trails around the Muir Woods and in the surrounding hillsides. A particularly good one is the Miwok trail at the top of the road.

* A short drive away is the 6,233 acre Mount Tamalpais Park, where you have a panoramic view of all the nearby cities, ocean, and bay (and if the winds are right - a few daring hang-gliders).

PEOPLE PLEASURES:
* Sausalito and Mill Valley are just 9 miles away and offer a wide variety of shopping, dining, and excellent espresso "hangouts".
* Take a drive along panoramic Highway 1. You will be treated to a scenic journey through old California towns, fishing villages, park lands and virgin beaches.
* San Francisco offers visitors the charm of a small town and the variety of a large city. A few noteworthy stops are the Cliff House, Fort Point National Historic Site, and Coit Tower.

THE PELICAN INN, Muir Beach, CA., 94965.

---

# CASA MADRONA
## Sausalito

MANAGER:     Dick Messer

TELEPHONE:   (415) 332-0502

LODGING:     Five cottages

RATES:       Cottage: $140 - 160.
             Credit Cards:  All Major.

Sausalito acquired its name from the Spanish explorers who discovered it in 1775. At the time, they found groves of willow trees along the banks of the stream, and appropriately called this area "Saucelito". Over the years both the name and the village have undergone dramatic changes, and those who visit todays' "Sausalito" will find, in place of a sleepy village, a trendy coastal town.

The hotel's grey-blue rooms stair-step up the steep hillside. The intimate cottages at the top of this incline are most appropriate for guests who are traveling with their furry companions. They are spacious and easily accessible to Sausalito's winding streets. Fragrant flower gardens line the ivy-strewn paths, with groves of evergreen, lilac, and pine trees swaying in the bay's breezes.

Located next to the Casa Madrona's country-style restaurant, the cottages command sweeping views of the San Francisco Bay. They all have distinctive exterior and interior designs. Your cottage may have a separate living room, dining area, or perhaps a kitchenette. Other features could include oversized beds covered in handmade quilts, braided rugs, wood-burning stoves, and comfortable rocking chairs. Special accoutrements are in evidence everywhere. Guests can expect to find bouquets of fresh flowers and bowls of fruit placed in their cottage, mints left on the bedside table, and a variety of personal care products in the bathrooms.

Each cottage has a different theme. For instance, La Tonnelle is renowned as the perfect hideaway for newlyweds. Its reputation could be attributed to the romantic wood-burning fireplace, enormous tub for two, and scenic garden terrace. The Calico Cottage derives its name from a country decor. Wrap yourself in the calico quilt, sit in the rocking chair next to the wood-burning stove, and watch the fog roll into the city. The largest cottage is the English Gate House, offering guests a charming sun porch, a preponderance of plants, and enough sleeping room for four.

The two new members to this collection are the Upper and Lower Casitases, located across the path from the other three. Stacked on top of one another, both have private decks with panoramic views of the Bay and Sausalito harbor.

After a busy day touring the "city by the bay", you may wish to return to the Casa Madrona and sample their complimentary wine and cheese. If you prefer to save your appetite for a special dinner, their restaurant offers a terrific California nouvelle cuisine featuring thick filets of salmon, moscovy duck, roast quail, soft shelled crab, and much more. The view of the bay from the picture window is almost as spectacular as the meal.

PUPPY POLICIES: Your hosts eagerly welcome lap dogs by prior arrangement. They ask that you do not leave them in the cottage unattended.

# FRISKY FRIVOLITIES:

* This is the land of many beaches, and chilly waters. Muir, Stinson, and Baker beaches provide hours of diversions for you and your dog.
* An exhilarating hike up the Miwok Trail (trail head in Tennessee Valley) will put you on top of the world. The ocean, bay, and northern California hillsides surround you.
* Hearty souls will relish an early morning walk across the Golden Gate Bridge. This is a fine way to see the San Francisco Bay. You may wish to climb up the trail/road leading to the Marin cliffs which overlook the bridge.

# PEOPLE PLEASURES:

* Visit San Francisco's Exploratorium. This science museum is known as one of the "finest in the world", as it allows you to experience, touch, and sometimes listen to the exhibits: (415) 563-7337.
* Your trip to the Bay Area is not complete until you have indulged in a "water" activity. Sailing, sport-fishing, and "Bay Cruising" are local favorites.
* Pick up a cable car by Fisherman's Wharf and ride it to the Cable Car Museum. You will see exhibits of the first cable car (1873), historical photographs, and the underground cable system in action: (415) 474-1887.

CASA MADRONA, 801 Bridgeway, Sausalito, CA., 94965.

# SAUSALITO HOTEL
### Sausalito

INNKEEPER:   Elizabeth McDonald

TELEPHONE:   (415) 332-4155

LODGING:     14 rooms

RATES:       Double:  $50 - 60,
             Double w/bath:  $70 - 80,
             Suite:  $120 - 150.
             Credit Cards:  AE, MC, and VISA.

The Sausalito Hotel will remind you more of an intimate European inn rather than a small hotel located in the heart of a California coastal resort. Elizabeth McDonald, your host, is certain to make you feel like a special addition from the moment you arrive to the conclusion of your stay.

Personalization is the watchword of the inn. This begins with the guests' quarters, each being individually decorated and named after a member of royalty. Victorian antiques fill your chamber's "nooks and crannies". Intricately carved wooden headboards, sparkling chandeliers, and beveled mirrors, are just a few of the furnishings. The windows are adorned with heavy, floor-to-ceiling draperies, forming a perfect frame for views of either the Bay or park across from the inn. A special surprise for history buffs can be found in the Marquis De Queensbury Room. It contains a bed once slept in by General Grant.

Depending upon your preference, you may select from either a private or shared bathroom. Shared baths are located between adjoining rooms, so it is not necessary to walk down the hallway to use the facilities. In keeping with the inn's English theme, the shared baths are conveniently marked "W.C.".

If you want to enjoy a bottle of wine, your host can provide you with a wine opener, ice, and glasses. After a peaceful evening of sleep, you will awaken to a Continental breakfast. Help yourself to the goodies (located in the lobby) and enjoy them in the privacy of your own cozy room.

PUPPY POLICIES: Your host gladly accepts small, well-behaved dogs, given appropriate advance notice.

FRISKY FRIVOLITIES:
* Sausalito is located on the San Francisco Bay. For those who wish to run or jog with their furry friend, there is a path that meanders along the water for miles.
* There is an amazing assortment of terrific beaches in the area; choose from Stinson,

Muir, Baker, or the St. Francis Yacht Club.
* The Bay Area is a superb "getaway" spot for those who have the wanderlust. Quaint towns surround Sausalito, and Mt. Tamalpais await those who enjoy mountain adventures.


PEOPLE PLEASURES:
* The Bay is privy to some of the best winds in the country, thus, windsurfing and sailing are favorite pastimes, for tourists and locals alike. You also might want to try a "wind" related activity. Sausalito Sailboards: (415) 331-9463 or Windsurfing Marin: (415) 332-2777 can supply you with further information.
* Take the ferry over to Angel Island (there are many hiking and bicycling trails in this State Park) or to Alcatraz Island (infamous prison).
* Enjoy the breathtaking drive along coastal Highway 1 to Point Reyes National Seashore. Your leashed dog will love visiting either the rugged North, South, or Limantour Beach.


THE SAUSALITO HOTEL, 16 El Portal, Sausalito, CA., 94965.

# THE SHERATON PALACE HOTEL
San Francisco

MANAGER:     Charles DeAngelo

TELEPHONE:    (415) 392-8600 or (800) 325-3535

LODGING:     540 rooms, 60 suites

RATES:       Single: $90 - 120,
              Double: $105 - 135,
              One bedroom suite: $225 - 250.
              Credit Cards: All Major.

The Sheraton Palace is a classic hotel in the romantic city of San Francisco. Some of the many famous visitors include Franklin D. Roosevelt, Ulysses S. Grant, Teddy Roosevelt, and Sarah Bernhardt, who was permitted to bring along her pet tiger. After that oversized feline's visit, your dog will have trouble rattling the management.

Ideally located in the heart of the financial and shopping districts of San Francisco, Palace guests can easily take advantage of the finest shopping, dining, and sightseeing the city offers her visitors.

The elegant bedrooms are painted in soft light blues, yellows, and off-whites which complement the high ceilings and finely carved moldings. In addition to the many standard amenities found in a quality hotel, you will also discover extras such as brass beds, antiques, decorative fireplaces, and vases of fresh flowers. The Sheraton Palace is a large hotel that is dedicated to preserving the gracious service and hospitality that we associate with another era.

Dining selections vary at this hotel. One standout is The Garden Court, which is a beautiful chandelier-studded dining room set under an airy and intricate leaded-glass dome. You will enjoy buffet breakfasts, traditional luncheons and tea in this fabulous room. The other restaurants in the hotel are quite good; however, we recommend that you take advantage of the fabulous San Francisco cuisine (easily some of the best in the country). Many of the the choice spots in the city are only a few blocks away from the Palace.

PUPPY POLICIES: They will accept your dog as long as he/she is well-behaved and not left alone in the room.

FRISKY FRIVOLITIES:
* There are dozens of scenic parks scattered all over the city that are ideal for walking your dog (especially in the Pacific Heights area). An ultimate stop for canine park connoisseurs is Golden Gate Park. (Of course your furry friend might be spoiled for life after a trip to this magnificent grassy oasis.)
* There are three great beaches to play on with your little friend: The Marina Beach, Baker Beach, and Ocean Beach.
* If you are a seasoned dog walker or runner, a scenic trip over the Golden Gate Bridge to Sausalito is well worth it!

PEOPLE PLEASURES:
* Pay a visit to the impressive M.H. de Young Memorial Museum (specializing in European and American art), and to the Exploratorium.

It is often referred to as the "best science museum in the world".

* Explore the many facets of San Francisco by driving or walking through Pacific Heights, Telegraph Hill, North Beach, Chinatown, and Ghirardelli Square. (Come to think of it, your dog might also enjoy this outing.)
* An informative tour of Alcatraz Island is a favorite among tourists and locals, thus you may find tickets can be difficult to obtain. During the high season, you should reserve tickets a month in advance: (415) 546-2805.

THE SHERATON PALACE HOTEL, 639 Market St., San Francisco, CA., 94105.

# CAMPTON PLACE
## San Francisco

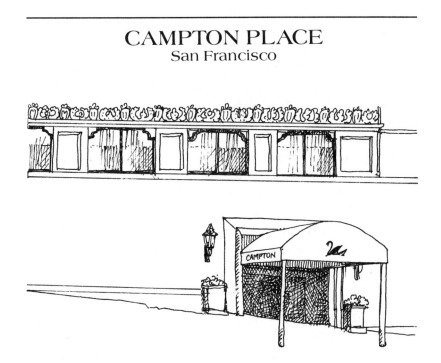

| MANAGER: | David Thorn |
|---|---|
| TELEPHONE: | (415) 781-5555, CA: (800) 235-4500, or (800) 647-4007 |
| LODGING: | 126 rooms, 10 suites |
| RATES: | Double: $140 - 200, Suite: $375 - 650. Credit Cards: All Major. |

"Where high expectations are quietly met" is the motto developed and strictly followed by your hosts at the Campton Place. This is the newest addition to the growing list of San Francisco's intimate, luxury hotels. Its winning combination of highly personalized service, exquisite guest rooms and public areas, and one of the finest restaurants in the country, all serve to make this hotel fit for a king, or queen.

It is also ideal for mere mortals who wish to sample a bit of luxury. Each and every bedroom is warm and inviting with fluffy peach comforters, thick, soft, earth-toned carpets, and overstuffed chairs to match. From your oversized bed you will find you can control both the television (hidden in a Henredon armoire) and the sophisticated lighting system. Brass is used liberally, from trimming the tables holding your fresh flowers to the fixtures in your bath (polished daily). Equally as luxurious as the bedrooms are the bathrooms, appointed with fragrant hand-milled French soaps and shampoos, thick, fluffy towels, and telephones (for the call that cannot wait).

Each room is similar in size, differing only with the addition of a small sitting area. Suites have a separate living room with wet bar, marble furnishings, and fine "objets d'art". All guests receive personalized treatment that extends far beyond the norm. The Campton Place staff will be happy to satisfy "virtually all guest requests, no matter how extraordinary". The incredible luxury and pampering you receive justifies what some may consider to be a high tariff.

PUPPY POLICIES: Odd, but true, the Campton Place will accept your dog if he/she weighs "less than fifteen pounds" (smaller than a breadbox). Those who fit the bill are going to be completely spoiled (rumor has it that "its a dog's life").

FRISKY FRIVOLITIES:
* Walk one block and you will be in the heart of Union Square, home of the finest shopping in San Francisco. Bring your pampered pet to Robinson's Pets at 135 Maiden Lane.
* San Francisco is a great city for walking. Chinatown is only three blocks away, while Nob Hill and the Financial District lie a leisurely ten minutes from the hotel.
* Jump in the car and drive to Baker Beach. Here your dog can run down the long sandy shore. At the far end, you both will enjoy the spectacular view of the Golden Gate Bridge and the nude sunbathers.

PEOPLE PLEASURES:
* Rent roller skates over by Golden Gate Park (Thrills on Wheels is a good bet) and skate the day away.
* Take the ferry over to Sausalito and spend the day shopping or the afternoon sipping a

Bloody Mary or two at the Alta Mira (great views of the bay).
* Visit Pier 39, on Fisherman's Wharf and then stroll along the waterfront. This is a great area for observing the street entertainers, shopping, or watching a presentation of the San Francisco Experience.

CAMPTON PLACE, 340 Stockton Street, San Francisco, CA., 94108.

# THE MANSION HOTEL
## San Francisco

INNKEEPER:     Denise Mititieri

TELEPHONE:     (415) 929-9444

LODGING:       16 rooms

RATES:        Single:  $74 - 150,
              Double:  $89 - 165.
              Credit Cards:  All Major.

If you crave a unique experience, love the mystical, have a fetish for eclectic combinations of antiques, and a desire to rub elbows with a ghost, then you will thoroughly enjoy your stay at the Mansion Hotel.

Nothing is "normal" or "ordinary" about this mansion. The gardens are filled with thousands of dollars worth of wild Beniamino Bufano sculptures. Inside, famous paintings by Joseph Mallard Turner and Joshua Reynolds are interspersed with murals depicting the history of the Mansion Hotel. Artistic treasures abound; one standout is an awe-inspiring stained glass window in the dining room, towering 32 feet above you. And the list goes on and on...

As you step over the threshold into the heart of the mansion, your senses will immediately feel a need to move into overdrive. Sounds of a Mozart sonata echo from within, interspersed with shrill comments from the resident macaw - Senator. The crystal chandeliers cast a soft (and eerie) glow upon the gumwood walls and ruby red carpeting in the foyer. A handsome, oversized, Oriental vase filled with fresh flowers, highlights the room.

The time to explore the public areas will have to wait though, because a Victorian garbed staff member has prepared a glass of sherry in anticipation of your arrival. The houseman will then escort you to your bedroom. As you ascend the stairs, the elegantly dressed mannequins and collection of pig memorabilia will surely catch your eye. Each of the bed chambers is magnificently decorated, thanks to the never ending efforts of your hosts and the "Ghost of Claudia".

Step through the bedroom door and your ears are again treated to a Bach or Mendelsohn sonata. Oriental carpets soften the mood, while interesting ceiling angles provide the perfect visual backdrops for the fine antiques, museum quality paintings, and Victorian lamps. Scrumptious candies and a vase of fresh flowers are sprinkled throughout your room. There are many special accoutrements available such as a fireplace, window seat, or private terrace overlooking the gardens. Your hosts will truly extend themselves to make your stay at the Mansion Hotel most memorable.

You can also depend on a fabulous array of culinary delights during your visit. French roasted coffee and fresh squeezed orange juice are a most delicious accompaniment to breakfast in bed. There is no need to leave the mansion for a superb dining experience, as a fabulous gourmet feast is served to hotel guests in the evening. This extravaganza is followed by a magic show and concert by "Claudia". (She has even been known to wander the halls late at night, checking to make sure you are tucked in for the evening. If you are unable to sleep, she just may challenge you to a game of pool in the billiard room.) Claudia, the staff, and other assorted "surprises" await you at the Mansion Hotel.


PUPPY POLICIES: Well-behaved dogs are indeed a welcome addition to the mansion. Please make advance reservations for him/her with the hotel.

FRISKY FRIVOLITIES:
* Lafayette Park is one block from the mansion. Your dog will enjoy meeting the other dogs, squirrels, and birds.

* The hotel is centrally located for walking tours of Union Street, Chinatown, Nob Hill, and the Alta Plaza Park.
* A stroll through the sprawling acreage of the Golden Gate Park, the Presidio, or Crissy Field will fill the better part of a day.

PEOPLE PLEASURES:
* The Japan Center is within walking distance of the hotel. Here you will discover many interesting shops and restaurants. Check into special seasonal events.
* Spend a few hours at the San Francisco Zoo. There are constantly changing exhibits, as well as the old favorites: (415) 661-4844.
* Take in either a professional football or baseball game at Candlestick Park, home of the 49ers and Giants. The stadium always seems to be very cold, so dress warmly.

THE MANSION HOTEL, 2220 Sacramento Street, San Francisco, CA., 94115.

---

# THE WESTIN ST. FRANCIS
San Francisco

MANAGER:       Robert Wilhelm

TELEPHONE:     (415) 397-7000 or (800) 228-3000

LODGING:       1,200 rooms/suites - main building and tower

RATES:          Single MB: $95 - 160,
                Double MB: $120 - 185,
                Single TWR: $150 - 170,
                Double TWR: $175 - 195.
                Family Plan available.
                Credit Cards: All Major.


The Westin St. Francis is definitely a San Francisco institution, guarding its scenic Union Square location since 1904. The hotel is grand, and can be somewhat overwhelming to first time visitors, but do not let this preclude you from enjoying its many assets.

We recommend the accommodations in the main building, if you wish to truly experience old San Francisco charm. The tower rooms are elegantly appointed, but lack the character of the former. Many of the chambers have picture-postcard views of Union Square. Through your window you can either people-watch or just follow a circling flock of pigeons. If you want to venture up one of the infamous steep hills, just hop on a passing cable car as it slowly clambers to its destination.

All of the rooms are elegantly decorated; some in rich red, others in emerald green, with the remaining adorned in soft earth tones. Bedrooms in the main building have ceiling moldings and beautifully tiled private baths. There is a truly magnificent collection of French and Victorian antiques scattered throughout the hotel.

The St. Francis has a number of restaurants on the premises, as well as a nightclub (a favorite with locals) called Oz, located at the top of the towers. You are also within walking distance of some of the finest restaurants San Francisco has to offer.

**PUPPY POLICIES:** The St. Francis welcomes your traveling companion provided he/she is very well behaved. There is no fee or damage deposit.

**FRISKY FRIVOLITIES:**
* Saunter around the Union Square area with your dog. This is just across the street from the hotel. There is usually some activity to entertain you, ranging from groups of singers to break dancers.
* Ascend Nob Hill (a huffer and a puffer of an excursion.), and visit the newly, beautifully landscaped, Huntington Park. Just across the street is Grace Cathedral. You may want to tie your dog to a railing and peek in – the church is truly an architectural masterpiece.
* There is an excellent parcourse and bicycle path (not to mention a long sandy beach) by the St. Francis Marina. You both will enjoy the refreshing breezes, while watching the windsurfers fly across the bay.

**PEOPLE PLEASURES:**
* The Westin St. Francis is only footsteps away from the best shopping in San Francisco. An extensive tour of Sutter and Post Streets will start the experience off on the right foot.
* The theatre in San Francisco is some of the finest in the nation with equally as talented ballet and opera companies. Check with the concierge for current programs.
* Fisherman's Wharf, Ghirardelli Square and the Cannery always provide unique diversions. These areas tend to be very crowded on the weekends, but if you "go with the flow" it can be fun.

THE WESTIN ST. FRANCIS, 335 Powell Street, San Francisco, CA., 94102.

# GARRATT MANSION
## Alameda

INNKEEPERS: Royce and Betty Gladden

TELEPHONE: (415) 521-4779

LODGING: Three rooms

RATES: Double: $55.
No credit cards accepted.

The Garratt Mansion rests on a quiet corner in an historic Alameda neighborhood that is full of Victorian treasures. The outside is painted pale blue with white trim. In contrast, the interior of the house has richly-colored, beautifully carved redwood walls, and hardwood floors covered with Oriental carpets. It is truly a visual treat.

When the Gladdens moved into the mansion seven years ago it was still a boarding house, complete with 21 residents and full-time cook. After the boarders left, the Gladdens were finally able to convert a few of the rooms into a bed and breakfast. They plan to continue the conversion to its ultimate conclusion.

You will find the bedrooms on the third floor of the mansion, and a separate second floor sitting room that has been set aside for your pleasure (visiting, reading, writing). All of the rooms have multi-angled ceilings, and vary in decor. Our favorites are the Hershey Room (tiny Hershey kisses and various other chocolate memorabilia are scattered about), and the blue room (#3), complete with wicker and antique furnishings and a cozy sitting nook.

The three rooms share a bathroom, which is just down the hallway. The Gladdens have gone so far as to stock it with shaving paraphernalia, aspirin, and anything else you may have left at home. For your bathing pleasure, there is also a ball and claw bathtub, complete with bath salts and other sudsy goodies. For shower "buffs", there is an adjacent stall shower.

Each morning a hearty American breakfast is served, and be forewarned, Mrs. Gladden does not prepare any one breakfast twice (no matter how long you stay). Thus, each morning, a different culinary masterpiece awaits you. Whatever your reasons for visiting the Bay Area, do plan to check into the Garratt Mansion.

PUPPY POLICIES: Your pup is not allowed in the mansion, but there is a converted house in the back that serves as a perfect doggie "sleeping parlor". Please bring his/her bedding, and do call in advance to make a puppy reservation.

## FRISKY FRIVOLITIES:

* Walk a few short blocks to Rittler Park on the corner of Otis and Grand streets. There are ample grassy areas for walking/jogging.
* Drive up to the Berkeley Hills. These are, for the most part, undeveloped. You may hike through the foothills or walk on the University of California at Berkeley's campus.
* Enjoy a pleasant stroll from the mansion to Grand Street. Turn left and you will shortly arrive at the San Francisco Bay. There is a tiny beach (dogs are not allowed), and a long trail (dogs permitted) running beside the bay.

## PEOPLE PLEASURES:

* If you are a windsurfing or sailing fanatic, drive over to the Berkeley Marina. Bring your windsurfer or rent a sailboat/board, and enjoy the brisk winds of the bay (up to 30 mph).
* Alameda has a wonderful walking tour, along with many other interesting "things to do". Your hosts have tons of booklets and lists of the town's highlights.
* Make a special trip to Berkeley and wander the length of Telegraph Avenue. It is a good helping of the 1960's seasoned with a pinch of the 1980's. Whatever your pleasure, you will truly enjoy the many restaurants, bookstores, and shops here, and in Berkeley's renowned "Gourmet Ghetto".

THE GARRATT MANSION, 900 Union Street, Alameda, CA., 94501.

# CENTRAL COAST

## From Half Moon Bay to Monterey

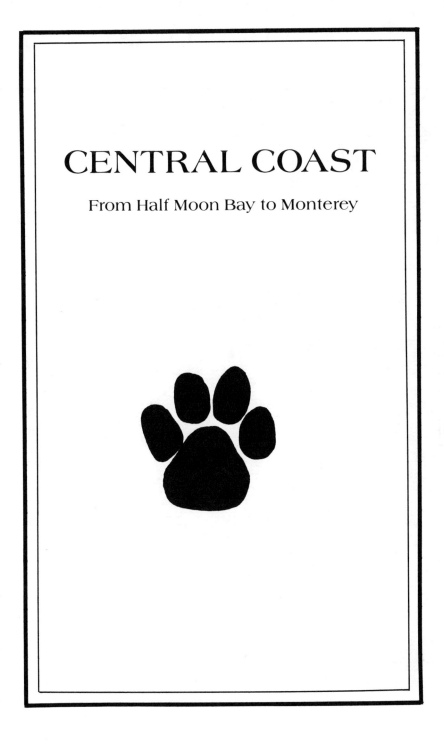

# CENTRAL COAST

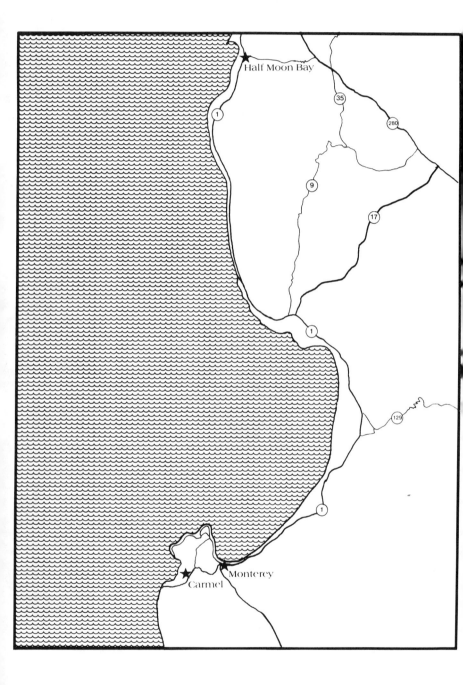

# HALF MOON BAY LODGE
## Half Moon Bay

MANAGER:     Pat Jealch

TELEPHONE:   (415) 726-9000

LODGING:     83 rooms and suites

RATES:       Double:  $56 - 74,
             Room w/fireplace:  $78 - 88,
             Suites:  $74 - 106,
             Credit Cards:  All Major.

The Half Moon Bay Lodge, true to its name, is located just outside of Half Moon Bay, nestled between the ocean and mountains. The town itself is a revitalized old whaling and lumber village, offering visitors a wide selection of shopping and entertainment choices.

Accommodations range from comfortable deluxe rooms with a choice of either queen or king beds, to luxurious suites with fireplaces, refrigerators, and wine coolers. The surrounding bay sets the theme for the lodge's decor. Glass lamps filled with shells, framed wildlife prints, and deep blue, patterned draperies adorn every room. Naturally stained wicker furnishings, beamed ceilings, and large balconies (facing the golf course or gardens) give each guest chamber the charm more commonly associated with a smaller country inn.

The lodge has carefully considered guests' needs, providing the extra accoutrements found in many first class hotels. Fresh flowers, coffee brewers, and delicious mints are placed in each of the rooms. The Spanish-tiled bathrooms are well appointed with heat lamps, double sinks, and a shower/bath with fragrant soaps, shampoos, and lotions.

Visitors will enjoy taking an afternoon dip in the swimming pool and whirlpool (enclosed by a glass dome). This pool area is surrounded by a number of potted marigolds, gigantic ficus trees, and ground ivy. The day would not be complete without taking a pleasant walk around the golf course or down the long sandy beach.

PUPPY POLICIES: The lodge charges $5/night for your pet and stipulates that only smaller pets can be accepted. (Sorry, big dog fans.) They add that dogs cannot be left alone in the rooms and should be leashed while on the grounds.

FRISKY FRIVOLITIES:
* There are seven beaches around the bay, not to mention numerous beautiful beaches down the road toward Santa Cruz.
* After exploring Half Moon Bay, take the scenic Skyline Highway over to Palo Alto, and Woodside. There are large parks, shops, and restaurants to explore.
* This is a very popular location for watching the migrating whales, frolicking otters, and playful seals.

PEOPLE PLEASURES:
* Championship Golf - Half Moon Bay Golf Links was specially designed by Arnold Palmer, and is conveniently located next to the lodge.
* Charter a boat at the Pillar Point Marina for a half day (or more) of deep sea fishing. One

other option may be to contact Huckfin Sport Fishing: (415) 728- 5677.

* Visit Ano Nuevo State Park; the site of the elephant seal mating grounds. Rangers lead guided tours.

HALF MOON BAY LODGE, 2400 South Cabrillo Highway, Half Moon Bay, CA., 94019.

---

# HILTON INN RESORT
## Monterey

MANAGER:      Robert Bullay

TELEPHONE:    (408) 373-6141

LODGING:      203 rooms and suites

RATES:        Deluxe Room: $75 - 119,
              Executive Room: $125 - 181,
              Suite: $250 - 400.
              Family Plan rates are available.
              Credit Cards:  All Major.


The Hilton Inn Resort has just been recently renovated, and the result is outstanding. The rooms are decorated in the earth tones, but remain spacious and airy. The first floor utilizes earth browns and beiges, the second - forest and sea greens, and the third floor - sky blues. All of the bedrooms have air conditioning, color cable television, a shower/tub combination, individually controlled music, and a private patio or balcony.

The suites are far more opulent, offering clock radios, wet bars, and shoe buffing machines.

We were particularly impressed with the third floor rooms, all of which have very large balconies (great for entertaining), Danish-style furnishings, and views of the beautiful flower gardens next to the pool. Most of the accommodations on this floor are suites, while the others are entitled executive king rooms. Although the latter do not offer a separate sitting area, they do provide the perfect alternative for the traveling family - a king bed, fold-out sofa bed, and a spacious sitting area.

PUPPY POLICIES: Your four legged furry friend is graciously accepted at the Hilton.


FRISKY FRIVOLITIES:
* Venture out on the walking paths that run alongside the ocean by Pacific Grove. This is a scenic and architecturally fascinating stroll.
* Enjoy the "Monterey Walking Path of History" (a detailed, self-guided tour map is available at the front desk).
* There are super running or walking trails in Don Davee Park (off of Munras Ave.), that wind in and out of the pine and oak forests.


PEOPLE PLEASURES:
* The Monterey Peninsula is the perfect place for oceanside golfing. For tee off times and other course information: (408) 624-6611 or (408) 375-3456.
* Visit the Monterey Bay Aquarium (one of the largest in the world), and learn everything you ever wanted to know about marine life.

* Bicycle on the 17-Mile Drive (weekdays after 8 a.m., you must be finished with your ride by 11 a.m. on the weekends). You can also tour from Lover's Point to Pacific Grove.

HILTON INN RESORT, 1000 Aguajito Road, Monterey, CA., 93940.

---

# MISSION RANCH
## Carmel

MANAGERS: Partnership

TELEPHONE: (408) 624-6436

LODGING: Meadow and ocean view cottages, B&B farmhouse rooms, and motel units

RATES:           Cottage: $73 - 79,
                 Bed & Breakfast: $54 - 66,
                 Motel Room: $45 - 49.
                 Credit Cards: AE, MC and VISA.


The Mission Ranch remains much the same as it was when the Martins first settled it in 1856. The original buildings on this 20 acre site are still intact, only now serve different purposes. The creamery has become a restaurant, the cow barn transformed into a party barn, and the bunkhouse now houses modernized guest quarters. The final result is an updated feeling of what Carmel may have been like 100 years ago.

The original farmhouse has been beautifully converted into bed and breakfast rooms, decorated in simple French prints and furnished with early American antiques. Our favorite guest room is #4 because of the unique second bed built into a high nook in the wall (accessible by step ladder). In the downstairs parlor, you can relax in front of a large fireplace where breakfast is served every morning to the guests.

The cottages are spacious and very simply decorated. You will not find the amenities of a four star hotel but you will discover clean rooms, picture windows opening out to wild marshlands, and seemingly endless open space. One group of these cottages is located near the eight tennis courts and the other is on a knoll close to the main building. There is also a cozy "honeymoon cottage" with a private backyard, separate living room, dining room, kitchen, and bedroom.

At the end of a long day, you might wish to take a short stroll to the award-winning ranch dining room and enjoy some great American home cooking. If singing is your forte, then join in with the local crowd, who regularly gather around the piano bar to sing 40's music.

PUPPY POLICIES: Dogs are accepted at the ranch without charge or damage deposit. The owners prefer that guests with dogs stay in the cottages rather than the farmhouse. (Unless some prior arrangement has been made.)

FRISKY FRIVOLITIES:
* Drive down the coast to Big Sur. Here you will find dense forests stacked up against the California cliffs. There are many places for you and your furry friend to explore along the way and while in Big Sur.
* Visit the bird sanctuary that is literally, just outside your cottage door.
* Follow the Carmel River down to River Beach. This walk brings you to one of the prettiest settings in the area.

PEOPLE PLEASURES:
* The Mission Ranch is within walking distance of the Carmel Mission (south end of Dolores Street). This historical landmark, built in 1770, is the most famous in the string of California missions: (408) 624-3600.
* Explore the many art galleries, boutiques and restaurants in Carmel village.
* Play tennis on one of the eight courts. Rumor has it, they are so perfectly positioned the sun is never in your eyes (in other words, there is no excuse for missing the ball).

MISSION RANCH, 26270 Dolores Street, Carmel, CA., 93923.

---

# DOUBLETREE INN
Monterey

MANAGER:     Mark White

TELEPHONE:   (408) 649-4511, (800) 528-0444

LODGING:     359 rooms, 15 suites

RATES:       Single: $80 - 118,
             Double: $94 - 132,
             Suite: $118 - 132.
             Special holiday rates are available.
             Credit Cards:  All Major.


The Doubletree Hotel is conveniently located, so guests may walk to most of Monterey's feature attractions (Fisherman's Wharf, Cannery Row, the beach, and the Aquarium).  Should you choose not to stray from this centrally situated hotel, there are over 20 boutiques and restaurants to explore in the comfortable atrium setting.

The rooms have all been tastefully decorated in earth tones and rattan furniture.  From your private balcony you will enjoy a view of either the pool, garden, or Monterey Bay.  Each of the guest chambers is cozy, soundproofed, and offers many of the amenities one would expect from a four star hotel.

If you enjoy a brisk game of tennis, there are three all-weather courts on which to play and a beautiful swimming pool in which to cool off after your long match. The temperature of the ocean is bone-chilling, and we recommend that unless you are seeking membership in the "Polar Bear Club" it would be best to remain by the pool.

PUPPY POLICIES: Your furry friend is welcomed as long as he/she is leashed and not left alone in the room.

FRISKY FRIVOLITIES:
* Beautiful running/walking paths lie right on the ocean (each over a mile). Try the ones along Fisherman's Shoreline Park and Pacific Grove from Pt. Pinos to Lover's Point.
* The Monterey Bay Beach is just east of the hotel and a fun place to romp with your dog. This is also an excellent windsurfing, sailing, and sunning location.
* El Estrero Lake is a pleasant jaunt from the hotel and a great place for dogs to meet and examine (not chase) the water fowl.

PEOPLE PLEASURES:
* Guest Services will help you arrange for deep sea fishing trips and sailboat rentals.
* Bicycle rentals are also available through the Doubletree. This mode of transportation is definitely preferable for leisurely sightseeing.
* Drive along scenic 17-Mile Drive - watch the sea lions, otters, wild deer, and of course the golfers. The Lodge at Pebble Beach is a "must" for either breakfast, lunch or a drink overlooking the 18th green.

THE DOUBLETREE HOTEL, Two Portola Plaza, Monterey, CA., 93940.

# LINCOLN GREEN INN
## Carmel

INNKEEPER:      Dennis A. Levett

TELEPHONE:      (408) 624-1880

LODGING:        Four individual cottages

RATES:          Double: $95.
                Credit Cards:  MC and VISA.


English country charm, coupled with the beautiful, Northern California coast, and a unique Carmel setting, give the Lincoln Green Inn an ambiance all of its own. The four cottages, set behind a white picket fence, are ideally situated in a quiet residential neighborhood. A picturesque English garden winds its way around each of the cottages, providing a plethora of fragrance and color.

The cottages are named after the characters of "merry old England" (ie: Robin Hood and Friar Tuck), but fear not for you will find all of the modern conveniences. A well-stocked kitchen, full bath, and cable television will surely make your stay more pleasurable. Personal touches of fresh flowers, a decanter of sherry, and a small library of classic novels also await your arrival. Best of all, you can enjoy all of this in front of a warm, crackling fire.


PUPPY POLICIES: The inn gladly accepts all dogs without charge. The innkeeper asks that your furry friend be leashed while on the grounds and not left alone in the cottage.

FRISKY FRIVOLITIES:
* The River Beach is only a few blocks from the inn and is a fun place for romping and swimming with your canine companion.
* If it is a little chilly or there are too many people on the beach, another great place is the Mission Trail Park (off of Junipero).
* Your high-society dog will surely want to stop off at The Barnyard for some shopping. (The Total Dog shop, has everything you could think of to completely spoil any dog.)


PEOPLE PLEASURES:
* There are many fine golf courses to choose from - Spy Glass Hill: (408) 624-1184 and the Old Del Monte Golf Course: (408) 624-3811. For complete information on all of the local courses and tee off times: (408) 624-6611.
* Enjoy cantering over the equestrian trails at Torro Park, Jack's Peak, and nearby Garland Ranch. In the winter you are permitted to gallop down the Carmel Beach.
* Try a little jogging or bicycling on the many coastal trails that lie between Monterey and Carmel. Bicycles may be rented from any one of the local outlets.


THE LINCOLN GREEN INN, Carmelo at 15th, P.O. Box 2747, Carmel-by-the-Sea, CA., 93921.

# THE LODGE AT PEBBLE BEACH
## Carmel

MANAGER:      Patrice Larroque

TELEPHONE:    (408) 624-3811

LODGING:      160 rooms and suites

RATES:        Guest Room: $175 - 195,
              Premium Room: $240,
              One Bedroom Suite: $290 - 435,
              Two Bedroom Suite: $480 & up.
              Credit Cards:  All Major.

The Lodge at Pebble Beach brings to mind the perfect union of natural beauty and luxurious accommodation. The original lodge, built in 1919, was Charles Crocker's Old Hotel Del Monte before it was converted to the showplace it is today. The 7,000 acre preserve, surrounding the resort, houses exquisite estates. Visitors will also enjoy the natural beauty of the pine and cypress trees along the rocky coastline.

The many rooms at the lodge have spectacular views of the coast from their first, second, or third floor balconies and private patios. Your quarters may lie directly on the 18th fairway or on top of a gently sloping hill. Regardless of the location, they will always be quite spacious and tastefully decorated, primarily using soft pastels and earth tones. Elegant contemporary furniture complements the decor, and is in harmony with the natural surroundings. All rooms have cozy sitting areas, some also have fireplaces.

Guests will have the opportunity to tee off on a number of infamous courses. Play on the same course that hosted two U.S. Opens and serves as the annual site of the Bing Crosby National Pro Am. For those who are interested in other forms of recreation, there are 14 tennis courts, 3 paddle tennis courts, a heated pool, a sauna, and over 34 miles of riding trails. In addition to the outdoor activities, you may want to take advantage of the lodge's Cypress Room (Continental cuisine), the Tap Room (casual dining), Club XIX (an intimate French restaurant), and The Gallery (family style with a great view of the the golf course).

PUPPY POLICIES: The lodge gladly accepts your little furry "country clubber". They do ask that you keep him/her in tow so as to not disturb the golfers and other guests.

FRISKY FRIVOLITIES:
* There are five trails for those energetic dog walkers, ranging from 3.5 to 9 miles.
* Enjoy trailblazing or fishing up in the Santa Lucia Mountains.
* Take a scenic tour of the 17-Mile Drive. Fun stops include Seal and Bird Rocks, the Ghost Tree, and Fanshell Beach.

PEOPLE PLEASURES:
* Try out the natural fitness program on the one and a quarter mile parcourse (begins at the Peter Hayes Golf Course).
* Get a bird's eye view, by airplane, of the California coast from Monterey to Big Sur. Del Monte Aviation: (408) 373-4151.

* Watch the undersea world frolic in one of the largest aquariums in the world - Monterey Bay Aquarium: (408) 649-6466.

THE LODGE AT PEBBLE BEACH, Pebble Beach, CA., 93953.

---

# THE HAPPY LANDING
## Carmel

INNKEEPER:    Jewell Brown

TELEPHONE:    (408) 624-7917

LODGING:    8 rooms and suites in courtyard setting (with honeymoon cottage available for special occasions)

RATES:    Double: $60 - 75,
Suite: $95.
Credit Cards: AE, MC, and VISA.

If you are looking for a particularly romantic spot in the picturesque town of Carmel, the Happy Landing Inn is your best bet. The two owners, Bob Anderson and Dick Stewart, took the original 1925 building and carefully restored it to its original beauty. All the rooms surround a central courtyard containing a white gazebo, small pond, and beautifully tended flower gardens with jolly statues peeking out from every tiny nook. The architecture is strictly that of a "Hansel and Gretel" fairytale, giving guests the wonderful

147

sense of visiting a land-of-make-believe.

Each of the charming bedrooms has a private entrance to this intimate courtyard. Once inside, you will find high-beamed ceilings, an assortment of handsome antiques, and Pierre Deux or Laura Ashley prints and wallpaper to enhance your cozy chamber. The added accoutrements of a decanter of sherry and pretty vases of fresh flowers supply the final touches. It is very apparent that a great deal of thought and tender loving care has been expended in both the beautification and preservation of the inn.

The personal service and special touches are what truly set the Happy Landing apart from the rest of the Carmel inns. Each morning when you open your curtains (a subtle signal), your host will bring breakfast to your room. You may also wish to dine under the gazebo or in the living room, next to the enormous stone fireplace. This delicious meal consists of fresh juices, coffee or tea, and a different baked bread each morning. If you are not sure how to spend the remainder of your day, Jewell will supply you with a plethora of helpful information on the Carmel-Monterey area.

PUPPY POLICIES: Small pets are gladly accepted, provided they are walked away from the grounds and not left alone in the room.

FRISKY FRIVOLITIES:
* The Carmel Beach is only four blocks from the inn. This is a beautiful soft, white, sandy beach to play on with your dog.
* There are a myriad of interesting shops and boutiques in Carmel, Monterey, and Pebble Beach. One store in particular will attract your dog's frivolous senses - The Total Dog, located in the Barnyard: (408) 624-5553.
* Superb hiking trails up in the hills by the Garland Ranch.

PEOPLE PLEASURES:
* Try out one of the local sporting pastimes: Golf: (408) 624-6611; sailing lessons, and boat rentals: (408) 375-2002; and the ever popular, hang-gliding: (408) 384-2622.
* Drive along the scenic 17-Mile Drive and visit the luxurious Pebble Beach Lodge.
* There is nothing better than a hot mineral bath at the Paraiso Hot Springs or Esalen (especially after a long day of walking).


THE HAPPY LANDING, P.O. Box 2619, Carmel, CA., 93921.

# VAGABOND HOUSE
## Carmel

INNKEEPERS:  The Levetts

TELEPHONE:  (408) 624-7738

LODGING:  12 rooms

RATES:  Double:  $65 – 105.
Credit Cards:  MC and VISA.


The Vagabond House was constructed in 1941 of knotty pine boards and brick. Each of these "English Country Tudor Inn's" rooms look out on a flagstone courtyard filled with flowering, potted and hanging plants, ancient oak trees, and several small gardens.

The rooms are fairly large and are furnished with wicker and early American furniture, quilted bedspreads, and an abundance of antique clocks. Personal touches abound, there is a small library of books, decanter of sherry, coffee maker (with freshly ground coffee), and a fresh bouquet of flowers for your enjoyment. For those who cannot resist a few of the additional amenities, we advise requesting a room with a cozy little fireplace, and refrigerator or kitchenette.

Every morning guests are invited to a filling Continental breakfast in the reception nook. Even if you are not in a breakfast mood, a visit to this little spot is worthwhile. The Levetts have an extensive collection of miniature books, antique clocks, and toy soldiers.


PUPPY POLICIES:  The Vagabond House welcomes your canine companion at no additional charge.

# FRISKY FRIVOLITIES:

* A short jaunt from the inn to Carmel Beach is definitely in order. You and your dog will be able to romp all along this white sandy shore.
* The Carmel area is renowned for its beautiful scenery, and what better place to enjoy it than at one of the local parks: Lover's Point, Pacific Grove, or Jack's Peak.
* Take a drive along the world famous 17-Mile Drive and visit the Lone Cypress, Seal and Bird Rocks and Huckleberry Hill.

# PEOPLE PLEASURES:

* After a long morning walking or bicycling around Carmel you may wish to take a trip to the Paraiso Hot Springs: (408) 678-2882 for a relaxing mineral bath.
* Skin divers may wish to explore the nation's first underwater trail at Point Lobos State Reserve. It also features a 1,276 acre coastal park that is filled with cypress and wallowing sea lions.
* For those who really want to rid themselves of those pent-up driving aggressions, take a spin on the Can-Am miniature race course: (408) 758-8629. If that does not do the trick, switch gears and visit the Monterey County Vineyards: (408) 675-2481.

THE VAGABOND HOUSE, 4th & Dolores, P.O. Box 2747, Carmel-by-the-Sea, CA., 93921.

# SAN ANTONIO HOUSE
## Carmel

INNKEEPER:    Dennis A. Levett

TELEPHONE:    (408) 624-4334

LODGING:    Private two and three bedroom suites

RATES:    Double: $85 - 115.
Credit Cards: MC and VISA.

This is a great old house, set behind a large hedge and surrounded by a spacious lawn. The inn boasts of spacious two- and three-room suites. Each contains a private bath, color television, and fireplace. One suite has a full kitchen (just in case you have an urge to cook) while the others have refrigerators. Freshly ground coffee, a vase of garden flowers, and a decanter of cream sherry complete the suite's subtle touches. As if these amenities were not enough to intrigue you, the innkeepers also display their unique assemblages of old toy soldiers, antique clocks, rifles/muskets, and fascinating miniature book collections.

Each morning you will discover the daily newspaper on your doorstep. You may choose to read this in either the garden or on your private porch, while enjoying a full European breakfast. The inn is so peaceful and cozy that guests often decide to spend their time just relaxing in the room. But should you wish to take a nice walk, the beach and town of Carmel are only a few blocks away.


PUPPY POLICIES: Your pure bred or mutt is gladly accepted without charge or damage deposit. The innkeepers do ask that he/she is leashed while on the inn's grounds and not left alone in the room.


FRISKY FRIVOLITIES:
  * The inn is just one block from Carmel Beach. The beach can be fairly crowded at times so head north toward Pebble Beach for a little more privacy.
  * This residential neighborhood is perfect for jogging and walking. There is also excellent shopping on Main Street. Carmel has a strict leash law, please observe it.
  * There is a parcourse in the Forest Hill Park. Both of you will enjoy the workout, if your dog has the patience to wait for you at the stations.

PEOPLE PLEASURES:
* Pt. Lobos Tidepools - Here you will see sea sculpted rocks, purple sea urchins, and many kinds of starfish.
* Scuba Diving - Follow the first underwater diving trail, which originates at the Point Lobos State Reserve.
* Soar over the local beaches on a hang-glider. Lessons and more information available from the Kitty Hawk Kites: (408) 384-2622.


SAN ANTONIO HOUSE INN, P.O. Box 3683, Carmel, CA., 93921.

# SOUTHERN CALIFORNIA

From Santa Barbara to San Diego

# SOUTHERN CALIFORNIA

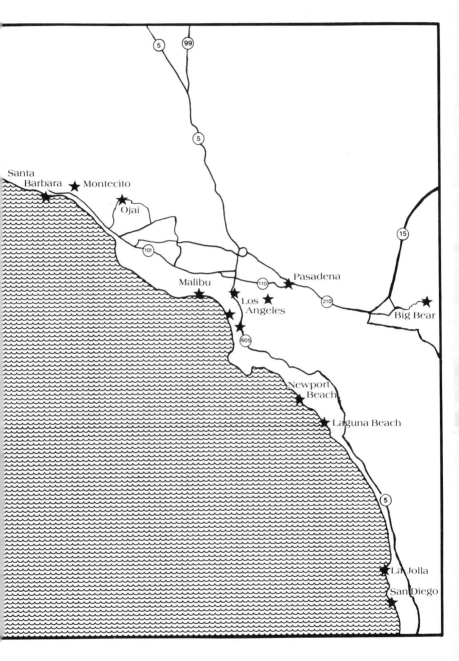

# MARRIOTT'S SANTA BARBARA BILTMORE RESORT
## Santa Barbara

MANAGER:     Charlene Nagel

TELEPHONE:   (805) 969-2261

LODGING:     229 deluxe rooms and suites, 78 cottage rooms available to guests with pets.

RATES:       Garden Cottage: $170-280,
1 bedroom w/parlor: $325-350,
2 bedroom w/parlor: $480-525,
3 bedroom w/parlor: $635-685.
Credit Cards:  All Major.

Since 1927, the Santa Barbara Biltmore has occupied an enviable position between the Pacific Ocean and the Santa Ynez Mountains. Perfectly manicured grounds, as well as an impressive list of room amenities, will enhance every guest's visit.

The cottage rooms are elegantly decorated in earth tones, complemented by pastel and floral chintz fabrics which enhance the luxurious affect. While relaxing in your overstuffed sofa, try to find your remote-control color cable television and refrigerator. They have been cleverly hidden in the armoire, creating an esthetically pleasing effect. The special touches do not stop here as the oversized beds have finely woven all cotton sheets, and the spacious bathrooms have thick, extra-large towels. The Biltmore makes a special effort to honor requests for bedrooms with unique features such as vaulted ceilings, ceiling fans, fireplaces, and/or private patios.

Recreational activities abound at the Biltmore. Swimming (complete with water exercise classes), croquet, and an 18-hole putting green should get you off to a good start. If that is not enough, an invigorating afternoon tennis match or refreshing bicycle ride through Montecito should round out the day. Of course, the concierge will also make arrangements for sportfishing, sailing, golfing, or polo.


PUPPY POLICIES: The Biltmore accepts your furry friend in the cottage units; however, he/she must be leashed while on the grounds.


FRISKY FRIVOLITIES:
* The scenic beach in front of the Biltmore is a wonderful spot for running/walking on with your dog. There are other furry friends who also frequent this beach.
* The Biltmore is set on 21 lush acres. Please feel free to stroll along the grounds. If you care to wander further afield, visit Palm

Park, a long strip of grass running alongside the ocean.
* There are a number of hiking trails in the nearby Santa Ynez mountains. The concierge will be more than happy to assist in planning your adventure.


PEOPLE PLEASURES:
* Horseback riding is a favorite pastime for many of the locals. The hills are covered with excellent trails for both the beginning and experienced rider. Look into the Gene O'Hagan Stable: (805) 968-5929 or the San Ysidro Stable: (805) 969-5046.
* Catamaran Cruises - enjoy a beautiful sail on the ocean on the "Double Dolphin", docked at Stern's Wharf, or go on a whale watching expedition: (805) 963-3564.
* Polo matches are held every Sunday (April through November) at the Santa Barbara Polo and Racquet Club: (805) 684-6683.


THE SANTA BARBARA BILTMORE, 1260 Channel Drive, Santa Barbara, CA., 93108.

# THE FRANCISCAN MOTEL
## Santa Barbara

MANAGERS:    Carmella and John Watkins

TELEPHONE:    (805) 963-8845

LODGING:    28 rooms and suites

RATES:    Double: $55,
Suite: $60,
Suite (with kitchenette): $65.
Credit Cards: MC and VISA.

The Franciscan Motel is ideally situated, only a few blocks from Santa Barbara's fine shops and restaurants and just one block from the beach. The Watkinses have expanded upon the traditional idea of a "motel", and have cleverly redesigned their rooms to include the unique "nooks and crannies" people usually associate with a country inn. Flowers, trees, and lush foliage abound on the property and in the central courtyard, which is also the location of a sun deck and sunken spa.

The rooms are cozy and many are furnished with queen- or king-size beds, fold out sofas, armoires, and fully-equipped kitchenettes. The Franciscan is a delightful retreat because of the attention to detail and the many personalized accoutrements. Each bedroom has deep aqua-blue colored wall-to-wall carpeting, vases overflowing with fresh flowers, and color television featuring HBO. The Watkinses are very gracious hosts and provide you with a quiet and simple vacation milieu.

161

PUPPY POLICIES: They will accept your fluffy colleague (small to medium varieties are preferred) for a daily fee of $5.


FRISKY FRIVOLITIES:
* There is a beautiful jogging/walking path that runs along the ocean (dogs are allowed on the less public areas of the beach).
* Santa Barbara contains many nice parks in the Santa Barbara area. Some of the more accessible ones include Shoreline, Palm, and Pershing.
* Enjoy a historic walk of old Santa Barbara on the "Red Tile Tour": (805) 965-3021.


PEOPLE PLEASURES:
* There are excellent windsurfing (Sundance Windsurfing), sailing (Santa Barbara Boat Rentals: (805) 962-2826), or waterskiing (east of Stern's Wharf) areas just off the coast.
* If you enjoy spectator sports, then drive down the coast to Carpinteria or Rincon Point to watch the surfers. Sunday is a good day to watch the local Polo matches that are played at the Santa Barbara Polo and Racquet Club: (805) 684-5819.
* Learn everything you wanted to know about native California plants on the lush trails at the Botanical Garden: (805) 682-4726, or make a special trip to see the many exotic animals at the Zoological Gardens: (805) 962-6310.


THE FRANCISCAN MOTEL, 109 Bath Street, Santa Barbara, CA., 93101.

# SAN YSIDRO RANCH
## Montecito

INNKEEPERS:   Susie and Jim Lavenson

TELEPHONE:   (805) 969-5046

LODGING:   38 individually decorated cottages

RATES:   Double:  $99 - 124,
Suite: $179 - 198,
Individual Cottage: $198 & up,
Cottage with jacuzzi: $259 & up.
Credit Cards:  All Major.


The San Ysidro Ranch first began as a cattle raising ranch for the Santa Barbara Padres.  From this time until 1976, guests such as Sinclair Lewis, Winston Churchill, Bing Crosby, Jack Benny, and

John F. Kennedy (then on his honeymoon) have all found solitude and serenity at this historic inn. When Susie and Jim Lavenson (he was president of the Plaza Hotel in New York) bought the ranch in 1976, they immediately embarked on a complete renovation project. The result is just short of miraculous.

Each of the remodeled cottages is different in size and decor, while fully meeting the innkeeper's "elegant but rustic" standards. Some of the rooms have been entirely reconstructed and now feature high-beamed ceilings, new bathrooms (with sinks set in antique bureaus or chests), and Franklin stoves or rebricked fireplaces. Other amenities of interest are the living rooms, modern kitchens, and porches or decks with private jacuzzis. When you are making reservations, please ask for the cottage or room containing your favorite features. We are sure you will find the ranch's staff and your accommodations to be completely delightful.

The recreational activities offered to you are just as varied as the room accoutrements. You may wish to spend your vacation horseback riding, hiking on the ranch's 550 acres, or knocking a tennis ball around on one of the three courts. For those who just wish to relax, we recommend a peaceful walk through the gardens or a dip in the swimming pool.

Early risers, will discover complimentary coffee and a morning paper awaiting them in the Hacienda Lounge, to be followed by a Continental breakfast. This is also the site of the "Honor Bar" (guests keep track of their own tabs), where the bartender in each of us has the opportunity to mix up those infamous concoctions.

One of the finest restaurants in California is within walking distance of your cottage. (It is so good that Julia Child often stops in for a bite to eat.) The Plow and Angel dining room offers a little of everything, ranging from tame to exotic culinary delights. A trip to the Plow and Angel Bar (formerly an old wine cellar) for a little music and live entertainment, will thoroughly round out the evening.


PUPPY POLICIES: The ranch welcomes your canine companion for a $6/night fee. He/she can even add a paw print to the special "dog registry". Note: They also accept horse(s) and supply the gourmet hay.


FRISKY FRIVOLITIES:
* The ranch's 550 acres of trails provide hours of adventure and entertainment for you and your canine cohort.
* Bicycle or roller skate (or walk) on the path running between Cabrillo Ave. and the ocean. Rentals are available at Beach Rentals: (805) 963-2524.
* Santa Barbara's "Red Tile Tour" gives your dog some great exercise and you the chance to see many of the most interesting local historical landmarks. Maps are available through the Chamber of Commerce: (805) 965-3021.


PEOPLE PLEASURES:
* Visit the Santa Barbara Botanical Gardens and explore the 60 acres of native flora and fauna. For a more exotic experience, you might want to stop by the Zoological Gardens and watch the monkeys, elephants, and birds frolic.

* There are daily trips out to the Channel Islands, just off the Santa Barbara coastline. This is a protected wildlife area where you will be able to observe pelicans, sea lions, birds, etc... in their natural environment: (805) 642-1393. Visitors Center: (805) 644-8262.
* After shopping on State Street (in downtown Santa Barbara), you may want to drive up to the Mission Santa Barbara. Occupying a lofty position in the city's foothills since 1786, she remains "Queen of the Missions".


SAN YSIDRO RANCH, 900 San Ysidro Lane, Montecito, CA., 93108.

---

# OJAI VALLEY INN
Ojai


INNKEEPER:      William G. Briggs

TELEPHONE:      (805) 646-5511, CA: (800) 252-0211
                U.S.: (800) 421-0000.

LODGING:        110 rooms, suites, and cottages

RATES:          Single: $135 - 165,
                Double: $150 - 195,
                Suite: add $75,
                Midweek Swing Holiday: $150-180.
                American Plan-all meals included.
                Credit Cards:   All Major.

Ojai is truly one of the few undiscovered towns in California, and it seems the locals want it kept that way. Situated in a valley 1000 feet above sea level, and ringed by the Sierra Madre Mountains, Ojai has only a few access roads – all of which are two lane. The drive is spectacular and certainly well worth the effort necessary to navigate it.

The Ojai Valley Inn is located in the center of this valley, surrounded by a golf course, green pasture-lands, and miles of trails. The grounds are beautifully manicured; the setting is tranquil. Whether you enjoy it from your guest room, out on the golf course, or from the swimming pool, you will never tire of the myriad of sun-reflected colors on the mountains.

Guests have several different accommodation choices, ranging from rooms in the Spanish-style main building to those in the four-tiered edifice perched on the hillside. Some prefer the cottages scattered off to the side of the main building. These open up onto spacious lawns, where you will spend many a warm evening watching the sun dip below the mountains. Each is air-conditioned and simply furnished with comfortable sitting chairs, a variety of single and double bed combinations, and modern bathrooms with separate dressing areas. Decorated in a number of color combinations, any of these rooms will make you feel right at home.

The Ojai Valley Inn is truly a resort, offering guests abundant recreational alternatives. There is, as mentioned, a golf course and 18-hole putting green, for those who just wish to practice their short shots. To top this off, you may also take advantage of the eight new tennis courts, croquet, heated swimming pool, and children's playground (with babysitters, should you need them). Lastly, the inn maintains their own riding stables. You can ride on hundreds-of-miles of trails or partake in one of the breakfast or barbecue rides. Both the town and resort are perfect locations for those who wish to either completely unwind or enjoy a more active vacation.

PUPPY POLICIES: The Ojai Valley Inn welcomes smaller dogs for a minimal charge of $2/day.

FRISKY FRIVOLITIES:
* Wander through the town of Ojai, where you will discover interesting stores, historical Spanish buildings, and Libby Park (the site of several music festivals during the summer months).
* Although the golf course surrounds the inn, there are many paths and fields to amble through with your dog, without disturbing the golfers.
* Lake Cassitas is just a few miles away and was the site of the Olympic windsurfing and rowing events. It is a perfect place to spend the day.

PEOPLE PLEASURES:
* Hot springs - enjoy the therapeutic waters of either Matilija or Wheeler Hot Springs. The guest services desk will be able to give you directions.
* Bicycle riding: The local roads are both flat and in good shape for those who are eager to investigate the rest of the valley.
* Venture out on one of the fabulous day hikes in the surrounding mountains (guest services will be able to give you suggestions).

OJAI VALLEY INN AND COUNTRY CLUB, Ojai, CA., 93023.

# CASA LARRONDE
Malibu

INNKEEPERS:  Jim and Charlou Larronde

TELEPHONE:  (213) 456-9333

LODGING:  3 bedrooms

RATES:  Single: $60,
Double: $75.
No credit cards accepted.


The Casa Larronde shares its coastal property with some very prestigious homes, on "Millionaire's Row" along Malibu Beach. This bed and breakfast lies hidden behind a wood fence. Step into the house and you will quickly discover its fabulous secret - a panoramic ocean view. Jim and Charlou have played off this ocean setting by furnishing their house with Hawaiian memorabilia collected during their visits to the islands. If you combine the decor with the Pacific ocean, you have a 4,000 square foot vacation getaway that is truly the best of both worlds - a California retreat combined with a layover in the tropics.

Three rooms are available to guests. All are decorated in tropical greens and Hawaiian orange with extra amenities including clock radios, color television, and wall-to-wall carpeting. The master suite occupies the second floor with floor-to-ceiling views of the ocean. All rooms have private baths.

The center of attention belongs to the living room with its wood-beamed ceilings, fireplace, and picturesque views of the beach and ocean through the vast expanse of windows. Sun pours into this comfortable room during the day, keeping it warm and cozy; evenings may be spent by the crackling fire. There is a piano for playing and a telescope for moon or people watching. Lush tropical plants fill the house with wonderful sights and smells, their beauty made possible by the natural sunlight filtering through the skylights. The healthiest specimen is a tree rising two stories through the center of a circular staircase.

Each morning a fabulous hearty breakfast is served to you. This delicious meal may range from special egg dishes to french toast. Enjoy this in the dining room or take it out to the beach.

PUPPY POLICIES: Your dog is a welcome addition to the Casa Larronde, provided you make advance arrangements. The Larronde's primary concern is that your "pup" not track sand in from the beach.

FRISKY FRIVOLITIES:
  * The beach is two steps away from the door. You and your dog will love the seemingly endless stretch of sand and water.
  * Will Rogers State Historic Park in Pacific Palisades comprises 186 acres of hiking trails, and a number of picnic sites. Will Rogers' house (complete with original furnishings), corrals, stables, and riding ring are open to the public: (213) 454-8212.
  * Take your dog into the Malibu canyons where you will have adventures galore.

PEOPLE PLEASURES:
- * The world-famous J. Paul Getty Museum lies minutes from the Casa Larronde. It contains extensive collections of Greek and Roman antiquities, and paintings from the Baroque and Renaissance periods: (213) 459-8402.
- * Visit the California Museum of Science and Industry, one of the largest technology, education, and science museums in the country, second only to the Smithsonian Institute: (213) 744-3411.
- * Spend a few hours at Olvera Street, the oldest street in Los Angeles. Since 1930 it has housed sidewalk stalls, restaurants, and shops selling Mexican handicrafts and foods.

CASA LARRONDE, P.O. Box 86, 22000 Pacific Coast Highway, Malibu, CA., 90265.

---

# MARINA DEL REY MARRIOTT
## Marina Del Rey

MANAGER:       Roger Speidel

TELEPHONE:     (213) 822-8555

LODGING:       283 rooms

RATES:         Single: $105,
               Double: $115, Weekends: $68,
               Suite: $275 and up,
               Family Plan: $75.
               Credit Cards: All Major.

The Marina Del Rey Marriott truly enjoys a perfect Southern California location. It is only 5 minutes from the airport, a few miles from the beach, and close to many scenic Los Angeles area attractions. It is also a safe distance away from the infamous smog and snarled L.A. traffic. This white Mediterranean-style building is so perfectly designed (many of the rooms face in toward the pool) that it creates a pleasant self-contained oasis.

The lobby and sunken sitting room are well worth a special note as they are quite small and intimate. If you need to meet someone, a perfect site is this cozy sitting area furnished with overstuffed sofas and lounge chairs covered in a pale blue chintz with scattered mahogany colored end and coffee tables. The attention to detail is quite extraordinary.

The rooms are decorated in what we like to call the "Marriott Red". If you have ever stayed in a Marriott, this subtle red is the traditional Marriott color. The decor is offset with tan and rust tones. The bedspreads also utilize these colors for an elegant floral print. Amenities are plentiful with individual climate control, am/fm clock radios, and baskets full of personal care goodies. The rooms that we highly recommend are the ones facing the pool. These have private patios (some with lounge chairs), and pleasant views of the lush foliage and pool.

As with many of the other larger, luxury hotels, please attempt to take advantage of the low weekend rates or family plans. These special rates make traveling fairly economical. During your visit you will want to enjoy some of the Marriott's recreational facilities such as the hydro-therapy and swimming pools. If you prefer a game of tennis, reserve court time at the Marina Tennis World (a short two minute walk from the hotel).

All in all, the Marina Del Rey Marriott will provide you with an relaxed environment for a weekend excursion.


PUPPY POLICIES: Your dog is always welcome at the Marriott.


FRISKY FRIVOLITIES:
* Walk from the hotel down to the Marina (10 minutes). There are an assortment of motor yachts and sailboats docked in this harbor. You will also find the ocean breeze to be refreshing.
* A five minute walk will bring you to an open, grassy park. This seems to be a favorite spot for chance "dog" meetings.
* Walk or jog through the streets of Marina Del Rey - it is a joggers paradise with its cool ocean winds.


PEOPLE PLEASURES:
* During race season, you might want to catch an evening horse event at Hollywood Park.
* Visit the La Brea Tar Pits which are the site of the richest known remains from the Ice Age. Admission is free: (213) 857-6311.
* You are in the land of Hollywood and famous film sets. Perhaps a visit to the Burbank Studios: (818) 954-6000, Disney Studios: (818) 840-1000, or 20th Century Fox: (213) 277-2211 would be appropriate.


MARINA DEL REY MARRIOTT, Lincoln Boulevard and Marina del Rey Freeway, Marina del Rey, CA., 90291.

# SHERATON PLAZA LA REINA HOTEL
## Los Angeles

MANAGER:      Ross T. Alexander

TELEPHONE:    (213) 642-1111 or (800) 325-3535

LODGING:      810 rooms, 23 suites

RATES:        Single:  $95 - 110,
              Double:  $110 - 135,
              Weekend Special:  $57.
              Credit Cards:  All Major.

    The Sheraton Plaza La Reina Hotel is located next to the Los Angeles Airport, but do not worry about extraneous noise because once you step inside the doors the sounds of the "real world" disappear. This especially holds true with regard to the guest rooms.

All of the accommodations are well-sized, but the design of certain rooms is substantially larger than others, creating space for extras such as a writing desk, king-size bed, matching sofa and sitting chairs. Unfortunately, these particular rooms cannot be reserved in advance, but please request one when checking in, as the cost is comparable to the other doubles.

The Plaza La Reina has clearly taken some additional steps to ensure the comfort of your stay. The basket of personal care goodies will make your hot shower a luxurious experience, and afterwards you will want to wrap up in the soft terry cloth robe. The digital alarm clock will wake you up on time in the morning (allow an extra few minutes to read the morning paper waiting outside your door). If you should have a flight to catch, a complimentary shuttle bus will whisk you off to the airport.

There are three restaurants to choose from at the Plaza La Reina, ranging from 24-hour service in the Plaza Brasserie, to nouvelle cuisine at le Gourmet, and fine dining at Landry's Restaurant. You may also enjoy reclining next to the swimming pool and sipping cocktails at the Plaza Lounge. The options abound, but whatever your decision, you are sure to enjoy a stay at the Plaza La Reina.

PUPPY POLICIES: Your small "pupster" is a very welcome addition to the Plaza La Reina. This is a city hotel, and you may want to make a special effort to make him/her feel comfortable with the Los Angeles "hustle and bustle".

FRISKY FRIVOLITIES:
  * You and your dog will enjoy a jaunt to Venice Beach, where you can just "hang out" on the boardwalk along with the rest of the locals. The sights range from roller skaters to true California "surfers", and much more.
  * Drive up to Beverly Hills, find an interesting section of town, and just meander through a neighborhood. It is an oasis in the cement jungle of Los Angeles.
  * Explore the UCLA campus. There are dozens of great areas for exercising you and your pup. Afterwards, the town of Westwood is a fun place to wander through, while enjoying ice cream or other treats from one of the many gourmet "eateries".

PEOPLE PLEASURES:
  * Fisherman's Village is located in Marina Del Rey, just 10 minutes away from the Plaza La Reina. This area offers great waterside shopping, an opportunity to look at the 7,000 boats in the marina, and the option to spend the day fishing or sailing.
  * Marineland is located in Palos Verdes, right on the Pacific Ocean. People of all ages will enjoy the entertainment and opportunity to see the marine life. Marineland also has a swim-through aquarium and a handful of the world's largest killer whales in captivity.
  * The RMS Queen Mary and Spruce Goose can be found in Long Beach. Plan on spending a few hours visiting this historic, luxurious ocean liner and the world's largest airplane.

SHERATON PLAZA LA REINA HOTEL, 6101 West Century Blvd., Los Angeles, CA., 90045.

# AIRPORT HILTON & TOWERS
## Los Angeles

MANAGER:      Lynn H. Montjoy

TELEPHONE:    (213) 410-4000 or (800) 445-8667

LODGING:      1,281 rooms and suites

RATES:        Single:   $65 - 120,
              Double:   $80 - 130,
              Suite:    $250 and up.
              Family packages and special rates
              are available.
              Credit Cards:   All Major.

The Hilton Hotel is determined to provide its guests with more than what one would expect from standard airport hotel accommodation. They have created a distinctive ambiance through the use of brass, chandeliers, beautifully polished woodwork, and creative greenery set within a full spectrum of pastel earth-tones.

The rooms vary in decor; however, they tend to have wicker furniture, plush carpeting, remote control television, spacious bathrooms, and nice views. The tower section is somewhat of an inn within a hotel, as it offers separate concierge service, a private bar and library, and luxurious suites. Furthermore, guests may take advantage of The Century Center Health and Racquet Club, equipped with racquetball courts, saunas, exercise machines, steambaths, and whirlpools. After a strenuous workout, you may wish to relax in the sun at Coconut Willies and enjoy a bite to eat or a refreshing libation. Perhaps you may want to treat yourself to a fine dinner at Alexander's, where the mood is enhanced with soft lighting, table linens, silver and crystal dinnerware, and an enticing menu.

PUPPY POLICIES: The hotel gladly welcomes the smaller, well-behaved variety, provided guests sign an agreement accepting responsibility for any damage.

FRISKY FRIVOLITIES:
* Two "wild and crazy" spots to take your dog are Manhattan Beach and Venice. There are a number of great paths and small parks close to the water for running and sunning.
* If you want to get away from the hustle and bustle of the airport, a scenic trip up to Mulholland Drive is well worthwhile. On a clear day views of the ocean, mountains and valleys are exquisite.
* You may want to show your furry friend some movie stars; take a drive up to Malibu Beach and park close to "the Colony". Once you get to the beach, walk up toward the row of beautiful houses. Who knows who you may run into.....

PEOPLE PLEASURES:
* Visit the NBC studios in Burbank or pick up a free ticket to an ABC television taping.
* The Los Angeles Zoo is worth a visit as it houses over 2000 animals who anxiously look forward to meeting you.

\* The theatre in Los Angeles is excellent and ranges from off-Broadway touring shows to local comedy clubs. The concierge or the Los Angeles Times will have a listing of all the current "happenings".

THE LOS ANGELES AIRPORT HILTON & TOWERS, 5711 West Century Blvd, Los Angeles, CA., 90045.

---

# CENTURY PLAZA
## Los Angeles

MANAGER:        William Quinn

TELEPHONE:      (213) 277-2000 or (800) 228-3000

LODGING:        322 rooms/suites in tower, 750
                main building rooms/suites

RATES:          Single: $118 - 138,
                Double: $138 - 158,
                Tower Single: $155 - 175,
                Tower Double: $175 - 195,
                Suite: $300 - 3,000.
                Credit Cards: All Major.

The Century Plaza is situated in the heart of a bustling shopping/theater area just outside of Beverly Hills. The new tower addition to the hotel opened at the end of 1984, and reminds one more of a small luxurious European inn rather than a deluxe metropolitan hotel. After spending over 87 million dollars on the tower addition, it is not surprising to find exquisite collections of imported rugs, hanging tapestries, and Oriental vases filled with elegant flower arrangements throughout the lobby and upstairs hallways. This floral splendor is particularly spectacular when set against the imported Carrera marble floors and pillars.

The tower rooms are impeccably designed with large sliding glass windows, opening up onto the private balconies overlooking either the mountains or Pacific ocean. Combinations of antiques, brass, and original works of art, will draw your attention into the room and away from the fabulous views. Soft pastels create a soothing effect, while fluffy down comforters and the oversized beds will surely warm your body in luxurious style. Each bathroom features a double marble sink, a separate tub and shower, heat lamps, and a telephone. Some of the other standard accoutrements are a remote control color television, two additional telephones, wet bar and fully-stocked refrigerator.

The accommodations in the main building are also sumptuous and share many of the tower room amenities; however, they do lack a certain degree of intimacy or luxury found in the towers. Whether you stay in the tower or main building, you are sure to enjoy the attention to detail and elegance at the Century Plaza.

The Century Plaza also offers a wide variety of dining pleasures ranging from the Terrace and Vineyard, to Yamato's or the Cafe Plaza. Each one offers patrons a delectable selection of fine entrees. Just recently, the Plaza completed the final touches on their exclusive La Chaumiere. Based upon the preliminary reviews, this dining experience may be one of the very best offered in Los Angeles.

Guests may also enjoy swimming in the large pool, practicing on the putting green, or taking a leisurely stroll through a portion of the tropical gardens. Whatever your diversion, rest assured your hosts will always extend themselves to ensure your visit is most comfortable.

PUPPY POLICIES: They welcome your little frisky companion provided he or she is well-behaved.

FRISKY FRIVOLITIES:
* A brisk early morning run through Pacific Palisades, or on the beautiful beaches of Malibu, is a delightful way to start the day.
* Drive over to UCLA (5 minutes) and enjoy a wonderful stroll through the campus. There are spacious grassy areas to explore (doggy heaven).
* The sidewalks around the hotel are super for jogging. But, if you crave a more natural environment then drive to Greystone Park (Doheny Rd.). It lies on over 18 acres of woodlands, ponds and floral gardens: (213) 550-4864.

PEOPLE PLEASURES:
* For those who are theater buffs, the latest films and plays are always showing at the ABC Entertainment Center located directly across the street.
* The nearby shops (especially on Rodeo Drive) feature the most exclusive merchandise in the Beverly Hills area.
* Universal Studios is only a short distance from the hotel. You will enjoy exploring this gigantic movie and television complex. Once inside the Entertainnment Center you can watch live shows being taped.

# THE WESTIN BONAVENTURE
## Los Angeles

| MANAGER: | James Treadway |
|---|---|
| TELEPHONE: | (213) 624-1000, (800) 228-3000 |
| LODGING: | 1,474 rooms and suites |
| RATES: | Single: $115 - 131,<br>Double: $135 - 151,<br>Suite: $262 - 600.<br>Specialty Suite: $715 - 1,834.<br>Weekend Package: $69.<br>Credit Cards: All Major. |

The Westin Bonaventure is in the heart of downtown Los Angeles, close to theater, sporting, and cultural events. Its five circular towers were designed by John Portman and if you look closely you will see glass elevators briskly transporting visitors up and down the hotel's exterior. Once inside the Westin, you will marvel at the myriad of shopping and entertainment features. The second through sixth floors consist of a shopping gallery, housing everything from boutiques and restaurants to clothing and jewelry stores.

The accommodations vary somewhat in design and size, but all are elegantly decorated, utilizing the subtle earth tones. Brass lamps illuminate the writing desk and comfortable furniture. This effect is further enhanced by framed contemporary art. The special accoutrements include fragrant shampoos and creams, bouquets of flowers, and potted plants. If you do not have a great view of the pool or downtown Los Angeles, you are sure to marvel at the aerial view of the lake and fountains in the lobby.

PUPPY POLICIES: The Bonaventure gladly accepts smaller, well-behaved dogs at no additional charge.


FRISKY FRIVOLITIES:
* Enjoy the ferry ride to Catalina Island, where you may fish, ride bicycles, or just wander through the town's shops.
* Enjoy the many Southern California beaches (Malibu and Santa Monica).
* Drive up to the Mt. Wilson Observatory in Angeles National Forest. This forest provides great walking paths and picnic sites.


PEOPLE POLICIES:
* Experience the Universal Studios tour where you will see the 420 acre movie back lot and learn about the animation process.
* Drive up to the Griffith Park Observatory in the midst of over 4,000 acres of park land: (213) 664-1191. Spend a star-studded hour or two amid the exhibits or experience the musical extravaganza at the nightly Laserium show.
* See over 2000 animals at the Los Angeles Zoo. Set on over 113 acres, there are five distinct continental areas represented, and a special Children's Zoo: (213) 749-2434.


THE WESTIN BONAVENTURE, 404 South Figueroa, Los Angeles, CA., 90071.

# HUNTINGTON SHERATON HOTEL
## Pasadena

MANAGER:        Denis McDowell

TELEPHONE:      (818) 792-0266 or (800) 325-3535

LODGING:        525 rooms and suites

RATES:          Lanai Building: $95 - 110,
                Main Building: $68 - 110,
                Suite: $130 - 500,
                Cottage: Prices vary with the
                length of your stay.
                Please inquire for package rates.
                Credit Cards:  All Major.


The Huntington Sheraton Hotel is located in a
picturesque residential neighborhood of Pasadena,

while also enjoying commanding views of the local San Bernardino Mountains. The immaculately kept grounds, highlighted by a floral horseshoe garden, have played host to the "rich and famous" over the years. The hotel is a tradition in the area, attending to guests' needs for over three quarters of a century. Whether you stay in a single room, suite, or cottage, you are sure to receive fine service from their highly competent staff.

The accommodations at the Huntington vary both in decor and architectural design. The color combinations can range from a sand with red and navy highlights to vibrant canary yellow and apple green. The beauty of this old hotel lies in the room features. You might stay in a chamber with four square walls and high molded ceilings or in one that is octagonal, with your bed tucked away underneath a bowed window. The simple old world charm of the Huntington is further enhanced by many modern accoutrements. All rooms have color cable television (HBO), air conditioning, and a lovely assortment of soaps and shampoos in the bathroom.

There are 23 acres to stroll through at the Huntington. As you walk over the footbridge connecting the Main and Lanai buildings, spend a moment looking at the murals of California painted by Frank M. Moore in 1932. If a leisurely walk is too sedentary for you, there are several jogging trails, volleyball courts, and tennis courts for your recreational pleasure. The Olympic size swimming pool will cool you off after a strenuous workout. If shopping is your favorite athletic endeavor, then consider visiting some of the area's most exclusive shops (located in the lobby).

Spend an evening unwinding in Arabella's, a comfortable spot to relax and have a drink. The view from the picture window is spectacular as it looks out over both the Horseshoe Gardens and the twinkling city lights. The Tap Room is a more casual and cozy gathering place for an inexpensive dinner or a drink. The Terrace, on the other hand, features a varied menu, enhanced by a view of the walking bridge and swimming pool.


PUPPY POLICIES: Big dogs, small dogs, skinny dogs, fat dogs: they will gladly accept them all. Please do keep them leashed when in the hotel and on the grounds.


FRISKY FRIVOLITIES:
* Lacy Park (1485 Virginia Ave.) is a beautiful park with a paved track encircling a large field. Your dog will certainly relish a jog through this tree-filled oasis (closed on the weekends).
* For those dogs and masters who love to go on long treks, a walk from the hotel up through the back streets of Pasadena will bring you to the picturesque Cal Tech campus.
* A nature lover's delight is a beautiful hike in the local mountains. One of the scenic trails can be found by driving up Lake Avenue to the end and following the road off to the left. A right at the flashing light brings you to Chaney Trail Road. Drive for two miles until you come to the trailhead, eventually leading you to a waterfall.


PEOPLE PLEASURES:
* Play golf with your VIP Huntington Sheraton membership at La Canada-Flintridge Country Club: (818) 790-0155, or on various other

municipal courses in the vicinity.

* A myriad of activities are available at the Huntington Botanical Gardens: (818) 405-2100. You may explore the 270 acres, containing over 9000 botanical species. The Huntington Library and Art Gallery exhibit outstanding paintings by Rembrandt, Van Dyck, and many other 18th century European and American artists.

* For those who want a real thrill, we would like to recommend a visit to the Santa Anita Race track to watch the morning workouts. You may also bet on your favorites during the afternoon races: (818) 574-RACE.

HUNTINGTON SHERATON HOTEL, 1401 South Oak Knoll Drive, Pasadena, CA., 91106.

---

# COZY HOLLOW LODGE
## Big Bear

INNKEEPERS:     Mary Kay and Mike Allen

TELEPHONE:      (714) 866-9694.

LODGING:        10 individual cabins that accommodate 2 - 12 people.

RATES:          Cabin: $40 - 115.
                Credit Cards:  All Major.

The Cozy Hollow Lodge is the ideal retreat for those who want to stay in simple, clean, and "spanking new" accommodations. The majority of these cabins were completed during this past year. All of the units are constructed out of white pine and feature a fireplace, queen bed with a brightly colored quilt, color television (w/movie channel), and full bath. The attached porches are terrific for picnicking and relaxing on with your friends.

The cabins are all rustically decorated with country furniture, throw rugs covering hardwood floors, and framed prints of mountains and skiers. Some of the larger quarters have very comfortable sitting areas and fully-equipped kitchens. For those who are planning on coming up with a large group, the Allen's have the perfect cabin. It will accommodate up to one dozen people in the two spacious bedrooms, and enormous living room with two fold-out couches. The kitchen is so large that all the guests may want to pitch in, but just send them back to sit in front of the fireplace.


PUPPY POLICIES: The Allens will eagerly accept your canine comrade, but are a little worried about potential damage to these new units. A refundable $50 damage deposit, is therefore requested.


FRISKY FRIVOLITIES:
* Big Bear Lake and village are just a short hike from your cabin.
* Wander the local trails and enjoy the winter wonderland or the floral splendor of spring wildflowers.
* Great cross-country skiing in the local area (telephone Ski Haus & Telemark for more information).

PEOPLE PLEASURES:
* Enjoy the fine snow conditions on the more than 14 miles of local Alpine ski trails.
* Saddle up for some horseback riding through the beautiful and historic Holcomb Valley.
* Take advantage of the many lake activities including waterskiing, fishing, windsurfing, and para-sailing.

COZY HOLLOW LODGE, 40409 Big Bear Blvd., P.O. Box 1288, Big Bear Lake, CA., 92315.

---

# SNOW LAKE LODGE
## Big Bear

MANAGER:         Joan Watson

TELEPHONE:       (714) 866-8881

LODGING:         17 time share condominiums

RATES:           Studio: $50,
                 Luxury suite: $85,
                 Adjoining bedroom: $60.
                 Credit Cards: MC and VISA.

The Snow Lake Lodge is a special exception to this book, as they do not permit dogs in the guest rooms, but have professional dog sitting friends who will lovingly care for your dog for just $4/night. The lodge is a luxury condominium resort that opened a little over three years ago.

The accommodations are so well maintained, they still appear new.

The rooms and suites are beautifully designed with all the amenities one would have at home or expect to find in a deluxe ski resort. The studios are spaciously designed with a large, comfortable horseshoe shaped couch, folding out into a queen bed. From the couch or sitting chairs, you can either watch the crackling fire or color television. The studios also contain a large fully-equipped kitchen, which comes with a microwave oven and a dishwasher.

If you would like a little more space, then you may decide to reserve an adjoining bedroom. Each unit contains a king-size bed, full bath, fireplace, and a television. Combine the studio and adjoining bedroom and you have a gigantic suite of rooms for at a cost of $85 per night. The most obvious advantage to staying at the Snow Lake Lodge is that these accommodations provide guests with just about everything vacationers could want in both luxury and practical amenities.

Each guest chamber varies slightly, but they are generally decorated in camel wall-to-wall carpeting, complemented by natural woodwork and large rock fireplaces. The Snow Lake Lodge also offers guests outdoor spas in which to unwind after a long day on the mountain or at the lake.

PUPPY POLICIES: As mentioned before, the lodge cannot permit your pet in the rooms, but would love to recommend using their professional dog sitting friend, just down the road. For more information please telephone Joan at (714) 586-5596.

FRISKY FRIVOLITIES:
* Depending upon the conditions, the town is a short walk or cross-country ski trek from the lodge.
* Hiking trails and picnic sights are scattered throughout the mountains.
* There are nice beaches on the north shore that are a little less crowded and would be fun swimming and sunning spots for you and your dog.

PEOPLE PLEASURES:
* The lake is a terrific place for jet skiing, windsurfing or sailing, and waterskiing.
* Drive on the Gold Fever Trail that covers many of the gold rush sites which operated from 1860-1875: (714) 866-3437.
* There is great Alpine skiing at many of the local ski resorts.

SNOW LAKE LODGE, 41579 Big Bear Blvd., P.O. Box 1146, Big Bear Lake, CA., 92315.

# IRVINE MARRIOTT
## Newport Beach

MANAGER:        Joel Rothman

TELEPHONE:      (714) 851-1100 or (800) 228-9290

LODGING:        439 rooms, 7 suites;
                54 concierge level rooms

RATES:          Single: $125, Double: $140;
                Concierge Level Single:  $150,
                Concierge Level Double:  $170,
                Weekend Special and Family Plan
                (four people) available.
                Credit Cards: All Major.


If you ever find yourself planning a trip to the Newport Beach area, and want to sample a bit of luxury – then think about staying at the Irvine Marriott. From the moment you venture into the lobby you will be overwhelmed by the spaciousness and opulence. This effect is achieved through the prolific use of glass, water, brass, greenery, and fresh flowers.

The "theme" is carried through to the guest rooms, which are decorated in the natural earth tones, ranging from sandy beiges to deep greens. Architecturally, many of the bedrooms are unique (particularly for a contemporary high rise); they are filled with all sorts of interesting angles, some even have slightly bowed windows.

The Marriott pampers each of its guests by offering amenities such as individual climate control, color television (with HBO), am/fm radio, and a complete array of personal care products. We know that your "pup" is usually very quiet; however, just in case he/she becomes anxious, all of the rooms are completely soundproofed.

If you do not mind traveling on the weekends and like to plan ahead, it is worthwhile to take advantage of Marriott's weekend special. It is called the 1985 special - $19.85 per person/night (double occupancy required). This is a great bargain, and only a limited number of rooms are available, so please make advance reservations.


PUPPY POLICIES: Your canine cohort is welcome at the Irvine Marriott. You may want to keep your pup on a short lead, when passing through the lobby, as there are a number of plants that are waiting to be knocked over by a friendly tail.


FRISKY FRIVOLITIES:
* The Marriott is in the center of a small park with nice, wide sidewalks and very little congestion, making it ideal for pleasant walks.
* Take a stroll along Newport Beach. Dogs are allowed on the beach during certain times of the day (varies seasonally).
* Lion Country Safari is just a short drive from the Marriott. You and your dog will enjoy the wildlife adventure (keep your windows closed as he/she may decide to hop out and make new friends with this little entourage of animals).


PEOPLE PLEASURES:
* Recreational outlets are abundant at the

hotel. There is an indoor/outdoor heated swimming pool, hydro-therapy pool, four tennis courts, and a health club available to hotel guests.

* Shopping sprees are easy at Newport Beach's Fashion Island, the South Coast Plaza, and Balboa Island (all within 15 minutes of the hotel).
* The hotel can help you make arrangements for deep sea fishing, sailing, windsurfing, or a harbor cruise.

IRVINE MARRIOTT, 18000 Von Karman, Irvine, CA., 92715.

---

# HOTEL MERIDIEN
## Newport Beach

MANAGER:      Antoine Vanacore

TELEPHONE:    (714) 476-2001 or (800) 223-9918

LODGING:      440 rooms and suites

RATES:        Single:  $115 - 150,
              Double:  $140 - 175,
              Corporate Rate:  $85,
              Weekend Special:  $85.
              Credit Cards:  All Major.

The Hotel Meridien is the newest and most striking addition to the Newport Beach skyline. There is only one way to describe this building from the exterior - futuristic. The design has no softening corners, instead the architects chose a series of sharp angles and nine stairstep levels leading to the sky. The affect is truly "wild".

Your hosts at the Meridien have successfully brought a French influence to the United States' "American Riviera". The lobby is bedecked with white marble, while the massive bouquets of fresh flowers intersperse color into this elegant setting.

The guests' rooms are equally as luxurious, decorated in subtle rose, mauve, and taupe tones. The sofas and the sitting chairs are comfortably overstuffed, while the fluffy comforters add the appropriate final touch to this elegant experience. The telephone system is probably one of the finest you will have the pleasure of using; it has the ability to control the room "environment" at the touch of a button. The hand-milled French soaps and shampoos, fresh flowers, and limited edition art supply the extra touches the Meridien is known for, the world over. Although the hotel houses over 400 rooms, the service always remains highly personal.

You may be tempted to remain "room bound" during your stay, but do try to take advantage of the swimming pool and the tennis courts, possibly followed by a therapeutic sauna in the health club. Afterwards, you may wish to migrate to the cozy, wood-paneled bar, followed by an early dinner at Antoines (overseen by a multi-starred Michelin chef).

The Meridien's weekend packages feature a single or double room for $85 per night. This includes a full American breakfast in their cafe and a complimentary wine basket. Whether you choose to take advantage of this special plan, or visit during the week, you are sure to enjoy being pampered by your hosts.

PUPPY POLICIES: Your small dog is a welcome guest at the Meridien. When making reservations, please inform them of your traveling companion.

## FRISKY FRIVOLITIES:

* The Meridien is part of a well-landscaped industrial park. There are wide sidewalks, large grassy areas, and many shade trees, which provide an ideal environment for dog walking.
* Bring your dog to the beach. (The evenings are best; however, do check the beach signs to obtain the legal hours for dogs to be on the beach.)
* Drive over to UC Irvine and explore their campus. There are acres of great areas for romping with your dog.

## PEOPLE PLEASURES:

* Visit the famous "Wedge", known as one of the most dangerous bodysurfing spots in the country. On big surf days you will see some incredible bodysurfers and some even more amazing "wipeouts".
* Take the ferry from Balboa Island over to the Newport Peninsula. Walk out to the beach or explore the boardwalk, after a delicious lunch at the Pavillion (beautifully restored building next to the ferry).
* Visit the Fun Zone next to the ferry landing on the Peninsula. This is an old fashioned amusement park with a Ferris wheel, bumper cars, and various booths where you may test your skills.

HOTEL MERIDIEN, Newport Beach, 4500 MacArthur Blvd., Newport Beach, CA., 92660.

# NEWPORT BEACH MARRIOTT
## Newport Beach

MANAGER:        Ray Kovacs

TELEPHONE:      (714) 640-4000, (800) 228-9290

LODGING:        337 rooms and suites

RATES:          Single: $97 - 127,
                Double: $112 - 142,
                Suite: $400 - 500.
                Weekend Package: $117.50
                Corporate rates and special plans.
                Credit Cards: All Major.


Occupying one of the more enviable hillside locations in Newport Beach, Marriott's Newport Beach Hotel and Tennis Club has magnificent views of both the harbor and Pacific Ocean. The lobby and other public areas are more reminiscent of the tropics than Southern California, with lush foliage and flowers growing from every nook. The sound of water cascading from the 115 year old, massive brass fountain (30 tons), completes this tropical paradise.

The guest room design varies in shape, while the color schemes are primarily red with hints of a sand tone. The baths contain an fine assortment of personal care products, and each bedroom is well-equipped with a cable television, clock radio, air-conditioning, and numerous other amenities. The incredible ocean views can be enjoyed from both the main and outlying two-story buildings. We highly recommend the latter rooms as they are more accessible to the outside world when it is time to take your fluffy friend on that "necessary" little stroll. The hotel's comfortable style and hospitable staff, will do their best to make your stay at the Marriott Newport Beach Marriott, truly enjoyable.

The recreational facilities are as diversified as the hotel's amenities. You will rarely have to wait to play on one of the eight tennis courts, or sprint for an available chaise lounge space by the swimming pool. In fact, the Marriott is in the process of building another swimming pool that will have underwater music. Finally, if you really need to relax, the hydro-therapy pool is a sure bet for relieving those tired muscles after a long week of work or a tough round of tennis or golf.

PUPPY POLICIES: The Newport Beach Marriott is happy to welcome your dog to its hotel.

FRISKY FRIVOLITIES:
* You may enjoy a casual stroll around Fashion Island (window shopping), or an excursion on the charming Balboa Island - a footpath runs around the perimeter of the island.
* Drive down to Crystal Cove, which is a few miles beyond Corona Del Mar (dogs are able to frolic on the beach during certain hours).
* Take the Balboa ferry over to the Newport Peninsula and spend the afternoon exploring the boardwalk, and enjoying the sights.

PEOPLE PLEASURES:
* Spend the day sailing inside the Harbor or out on the ocean. (You can sometimes bring

your dog - just inquire with the concierge.)
* Lido Island is only a few minutes away. Here you will discover boutiques galore, excellent restaurants, and beautiful homes.
* Rent bicycles or mopeds (the concierge will be able to supply you with more information) and explore Newport Beach. There are a few hills for the hearty but it is mostly flat, for those who like to peddle or coast along at a more leisurely pace.

NEWPORT BEACH MARRIOTT HOTEL & TENNIS CLUB, 900 Newport Center Drive, Newport Beach, CA., 92660.

---

# CARRIAGE HOUSE
## Laguna Beach

INNKEEPER:     Dee Taylor

TELEPHONE:     (714) 494-8945

LODGING:       Six rooms and suites

RATES:         Double: $70,
               Suite: $85 - 95.
               No credit cards accepted.

The Carriage House is a delightful surprise that will surely fulfill all visitors' expectations. The inn is situated in a residential neighborhood, but also lies in close proximity to both the beach and town. The Taylors purchased this American Colonial "saltbox" seven years ago. Since then, they have painted it blue-grey, and planted the central brick courtyard with a wild assortment of interesting plants, flowers, and trees. You will marvel at the enormous bird cage (much as their cat does) which houses a dozen or so canaries and finches. Whether your bedroom is placed on the courtyard level or upstairs off of the wrap around porch, you will thoroughly appreciate the personal touches made to your individually appointed room.

Most of the chambers are filled with beautiful antiques left to the Taylors by their "Grandma Bean". They have added their personal decorative flair, that gives each room a unique theme all of its own. One is appointed in a Victorian motif, another is French country, and a third definitely has a touch of the Orient. The suites have their own private sitting rooms, a kitchen, and separate bedroom (some have two bedrooms). The quarters are painted in various crisp colors such as aqua blue, cranberry, tropical green, canary yellow, or coral.

Some of the many amenities visitors may find in their rooms are ceiling fans, antique quilts covering sturdy brass beds, crackling fireplaces, and window seats. You may be lucky enough to take a bubble bath in an antique claw foot tub. After relaxing in this special retreat, you will surely notice the other pleasing personal touches such as fresh flowers, potpourri, and a basket of complimentary wine and fruit.


PUPPY POLICIES: The innkeepers will welcome your furry companion without charge, provided they are "lap dogs" and very well-behaved.

FRISKY FRIVOLITIES:
* There are several great local beaches. They do have dog restrictions that vary seasonally from beach to beach - please check the signs.
* Newport Beach and Lido Island are several miles away from Laguna Beach. Lido is a particularly good area for walking through and exploring. The shops are interesting and the houses are beautiful.
* Explore the foothills behind Laguna Beach. There are miles of undeveloped fields that would be fun to run through with your dog.


PEOPLE PLEASURES:
* Laguna Beach is a terrific area for sailing, boating, or windsurfing. You will definitely improve your tan in the secluded coves.
* A 20 minute drive will bring you to either Disneyland: (714) 999-4000 or Knott's Berry Farm: (714) 827-1776 amusement parks.
* The world famous Laguna Beach Arts Festival is held every August. You may purchase the fine selections of arts and crafts that are exhibited in the many booths. You will also be treated to the live reenactments of famous paintings at the Pageant of the Masters.

THE CARRIAGE HOUSE, 1322 Catalina Street, Laguna Beach, CA., 92651.

# THE INN AT RANCHO SANTA FE
## San Diego

INNKEEPERS:    Mr. and Mrs. George Richardson

TELEPHONE:    (619) 756-1131

LODGING:    15 cottages with 10-15 room/suites
per cottage.

RATES:    Double Main Building:  $55 - 95,
Double Cottage:  $80 - 110,
Garden Cottage:  $55 - 230,
Private homes are available.
Credit Cards:  All Major.

The Inn at Rancho Santa Fe is an exclusive
retreat for those who need to get away from the
hustle and bustle of everyday life.  It functions as
a full service resort, offering two championship
golf courses, three new tennis courts, a swimming
pool, and a croquet course.  Recreational activities
aside, you will find the inn most conducive to
quiet contemplation among the acres of eucalyptus
trees, bougainvillea, and ivy-lined pathways.

The cottages, which contain between two and
ten rooms, offer a wide selection of amenities. The
rooms are individually decorated, although primary
colors tend to be combinations of pastel yellow and
green, or deep red and blue.  Each guest room is
simply and attractively furnished with wicker and
overstuffed floral chintz sofas and chairs.  We are
sure you will also enjoy basking in the sun on
your private terrace.   The kitchen and wet bar
are perfect additions for people who like to cook
or entertain at home.  On the other hand, you
may just want to relax in front of a crackling fire
with a good book. For those who desire even more
privacy and space, there are a number of private
residences that become available when the owners

are out of town. These are adjacent to the inn and offer full hotel services.

The inn has a wide assortment of culinary experiences to choose from, such as the Garden Room (breakfast, lunch and dinner), the Vintage Room (cocktails), the Patio Terrace (dancing on weekends), and the Library (for elegant private parties). Even with all of these options, everyone ultimately migrates into the living room, where they find family antiques, comfortable couches, an enormous wood-burning fireplace, and best of all, a ideal atmosphere for making new friends.

PUPPY POLICIES: The inn welcomes your furry friend at an extra charge of $10/day. They also request that there be only one dog per room.

FRISKY FRIVOLITIES:
* Del Mar Beach - The inn has a private beach cottage that guests may utilize while frolicking by the ocean.
* Enjoy pleasant walks through Rancho Santa Fe's shopping area and on the inn's 20 acres.
* Drive over to Mission Bay. There are two islands with facilities for picnicking, and miles of shoreline for swimming and boating.

PEOPLE PLEASURES:
* Hot air ballooning is available in Del Mar Valley through the "Heaven on Earth Tours". Afterwards, watch the champagne flow and munch on hors d'oeuvres: (619) 336-6250.
* Visit the Wild Animal Park. A portion of the tour includes an hour-long monorail ride over arid plains where you will observe over 2,200

animals roaming the 1,800 acre, naturally recreated environment.
* Visit the Aero-Space Museum in San Diego. An outstanding collection of historic aircraft are on display: (619) 234-8291.


THE INN AT RANCHO SANTA FE, P.O. Box 869, Rancho Santa Fe, CA., 92067.

---

# LA JOLLA PALMS INN
## La Jolla


INNKEEPERS: Mary and Phil Sweeney

TELEPHONE: (619) 454-7101

ROOMS: 60 rooms and suites

RATES: Double: $49 - 69,
Double w/kitchen: $69 - 79.
Credit Cards: All Major.

The La Jolla Palms Inn is situated within walking distance of many of La Jolla's beautiful beaches, and only a mile or so from an eclectic selection of excellent restaurants and shops. The inn is located on a rather busy street, but any noise quickly fades away as you enter a quiet and peaceful courtyard. This area, as it turns out, is the primary focal point for the surrounding guest rooms. Our favorite rooms are those around the pool and jacuzzi - of course they are also the first to be reserved, so it might be wise to telephone the inn in advance to indicate your preference.

Yet another grouping of rooms encircles a second courtyard. These are also very cozy but do not offer the same charm as the former. A third cluster of guest quarters is located in a three story main building that looks out onto the street, but has nice ocean views.

The accommodations are relatively spacious and have been tastefully decorated with a deep, forest-green carpeting. The upholstery and bed comforters utilize tan, blue, and green color combinations which complement the surrounding scenery. The La Jolla Palms Inn outshines other small hotels with its attention to the special amenities. While the rooms are not elegant, each does offer a color television (cable) and am/fm radio. The bathrooms are spacious, clean, and provide you with an generous supply of quality personal care products.

Each morning the innkeepers proudly serve a delicious complimentary Continental breakfast in the reception area. If you prefer to sleep late and dine on your home cooking, there are rooms available with kitchen facilities.

PUPPY POLICIES: The inn gladly welcomes your dog without charge or damage deposit.

FRISKY FRIVOLITIES:
* Visit the Wind N' Sea Beach - your dog is allowed on the beach after 6 p.m. (on a leash).
* Drive over to the University of San Diego and enjoy a long walk/run while exploring this beautiful campus.
* Whale watch on the beautiful cliffs at Torrey Pines National Reserve (south of Del Mar).

This is also a terrific spot for you and your pup to picnic, sunbathe, or hike.

PEOPLE PLEASURES:
* Shopping, shopping, shopping.......La Jolla truly lives up to its name "The Jewel", when it comes to finding every type of trendy shop. You will discover interesting specialty clothing, food, and gift stores along Girard, Prospect, and other adjacent streets.
* Scripps Institute of Oceanography - Aquarium and Museum is located on the UC San Diego campus. Fascinating exhibits of sharks, sea tortises, eels, and various other exotic marine creatures will keep you here for hours.
* Test your golf swing at the Torrey Pines Municipal Golf Course. For tee off times and other course information: (619) 453-0380.

LA JOLLA PALMS INN, 6705 La Jolla Blvd., San Diego, CA., 92037.

---

# SCRIPPS INN
## La Jolla

INNKEEPERS: Kathleen and Earl Willett

TELEPHONE: (619) 454-3391

LODGING: 14 rooms

RATES: Double (High Season): $76 - 105, Double (Low Season): $61 - 90. Credit Cards: AE, MC, and VISA.

Located atop the cliffs directly above the pounding surf, the Scripps Inn is privy to one of the finest views of the Pacific ocean in all of La Jolla. The inn resembles a motel from the outside, but that feeling immediately changes once you step inside your room.

Each guest accommodation is quite charmingly decorated in French country fabrics and soft coral tones. Bright bouquets of flowers have been hand stenciled on the bureaus; one room even having a whimsical little pig painted on the wall. The special touches abound, with an added assortment of creature comforts. Color cable television, direct dial telephones, and small refrigerators are found in each unit. White cotton couches, while great for relaxing, also double as queen beds. There are various room designs to choose from; some house king beds (three have sets of doubles), others are suites with adjoining sitting rooms and kitchens. You may even curl up in front of the fireplace in two of the bedrooms, and listen to the pounding surf.

In the morning, you will enjoy a Continental breakfast of assorted juices, coffee or tea, and bakery fresh croissants (the very lightest). Your hosts, the Willetts, go well out of their way to make you feel comfortable and to ensure that your stay at the Scripps Inn is a memorable and special experience.

PUPPY POLICIES: Your medium-size "pupster" is welcome, but please call in advance as people and dog reservations are required.

FRISKY FRIVOLITIES:
  * Step outside your door and walk on the green

belt that stretches for miles along the ocean in both directions. This is a wonderfully scenic jaunt for both you and your dog.
* Visit any of the nearby beaches. Leashed dogs are allowed to "hit the beach" early in the morning and after 6 p.m.
* Take a trip out to Whale View Point, just south of the inn and watch the Grey Whales during their seasonal migration.


PEOPLE PLEASURES:
* The La Jolla Museum of Contemporary Art is a half block from the inn. This museum houses some of the most important collections in the West, and is well known for its showcase of industrial design.
* A short two minute walk will bring you to the center of the finest shopping and restaurants in the area.
* The Comedy Store on Pearl Street is a great place for howling or giggling: (619) 454-9176.


THE SCRIPPS INN, 555 Coast Blvd. South, La Jolla, CA., 92037.

# HALF MOON INN
## San Diego

MANAGER:     Richard Bartel

TELEPHONE:   (619) 224-3411

LODGING:     136 rooms and suites

RATES:       Single: $65 - 125,
             Double: $85 - 145,
             Luxury Suite: $175 - 250.
             Credit Cards: All Major.


    The Half Moon Inn is located only a few minutes away from downtown San Diego on Shelter Island. The grounds are modeled after a Hawaiian setting with tumbling waterfalls, lush tropical foliage, and a sparkling swimming pool creating this tranquil mood.

211

The guests' accommodations are interspersed throughout these fertile surroundings. The rooms are spacious with wood-beamed ceilings, naturally finished rattan furniture, and sliding glass doors opening out to private patios or porches. Some of the best views are from the rooms overlooking the harbor; these also appear to be a little newer and more private. Color combinations vary, but the ocean motif is used throughout, even down to the the shell design on the bedspreads.

Most of the fun lies in the San Diego sun. As a guest of the inn, you may utilize the private marina, laze by the pool, or unwind in the hot whirlpool spa. There is also a putting green a few steps away from your room. The combination of a helpful staff, cozy rooms, and a variety of recreational activities will make your stay at the Half Moon Inn a complete delight.

PUPPY POLICIES: Your hosts welcome your canine traveler and charge $15 to cover the specialized cleaning service.

FRISKY FRIVOLITIES:
- * There is a small park in front of the hotel, next to a long coastal walkway; it is perfect for a stroll or an enervating jog. This is also an ideal spot for trying your luck fishing for rock cod.
- * Discover San Diego's Old Town, an historical section that has been completely restored to its 1880's charm.
- * For those "park crazy" dogs, we recommend a few that are well worth visiting: Presidio, Mission Bay, and Balboa Parks.

PEOPLE PLEASURES:
* The world famous San Diego Zoo has a little something for "kids" of all ages. Learn about over 3200 different kinds of animals during these informative tours.
* "A Beautiful Morning Ballooning Company" is a terrific way to see this spectacular region. Advance reservations are necessary.
* For those who would rather be a little more earthbound, take part in an exhilarating horseback riding expedition through the San Diego hills. Poway Stables: (619) 748-4179.


THE HALF MOON INN, 2303 Shelter Island Circle, San Diego, CA., 92106.

# THE DESERT

## From Palm Springs to Indio

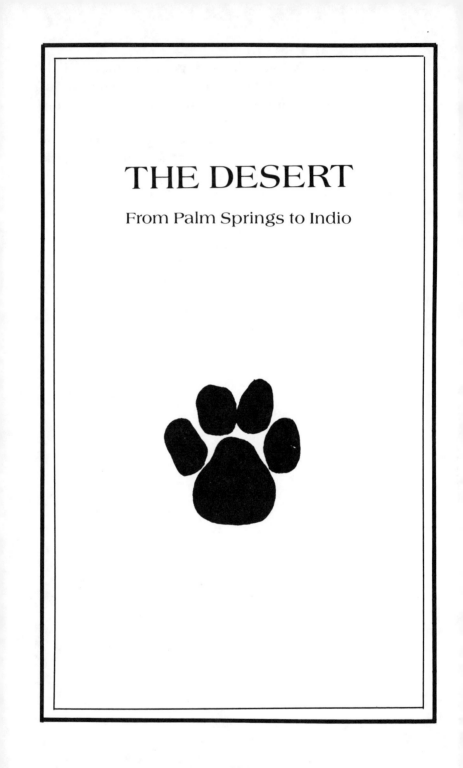

# THE DESERT

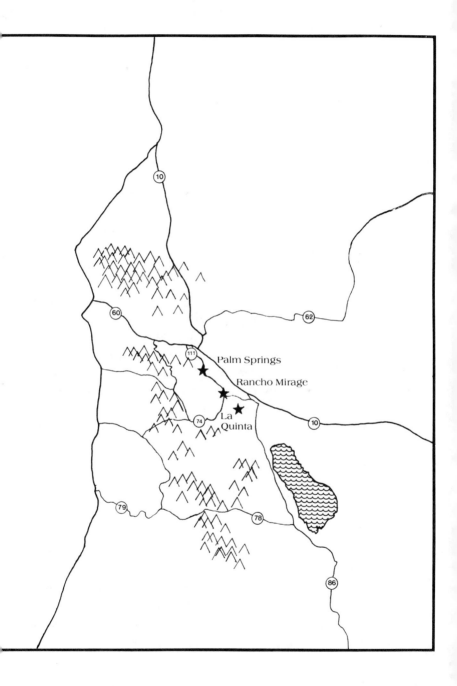

# RACQUET CLUB OF PALM SPRINGS
## Palm Springs

INNKEEPER:     Tom Ranck

TELEPHONE:    (619) 325-1281 or (800) 367-0946

LODGING:      170 rooms and suites

RATES:         Double:  $105 - 140,
               Double w/kitchen:  $145 - 165,
               Suite:  $205 - 335,
               Luxury suite:  $365 - 425.
               Credit Cards:  All Major.

The Racquet Club of Palm Springs is truly an institution. Some people may even remember when Charlie Farrell and Ralph Bellamy bought it in the early 1930's. Or perhaps they watched it become the "in" place for the Hollywood stars in the years that followed. Cary Grant, Marilyn Monroe, Clark Gable, Spencer Tracy and Frank Sinatra all used to visit the club because of its casual, yet personalized service. In this respect, nothing has changed over the last 50 years.

The rooms have been refurbished a few times over the decades; today you may choose from a variety of quarters. The Mediterranean-styled villas, which sit on the back edge of the 25 acres, are one option. These rooms are a little older than the others, and the surrounding foliage has flourished beautifully around them. Thus, guests have the sensation of visiting the tropics rather than an arid desert. Once inside, you will find the rooms are individually decorated, luxuriously appointed, and extremely spacious. If the need arises, you may request a room with a separate living room or kitchen.

The newest additions to the club are the condominiums which guard the front edge of the property. High ceilings, vast amounts of glass, and private patios collectively project a different theme from the Villas. Their dazzling openness is perfectly softened through the use of colors such as dusky rose, blush, and other pastel tones.

The rooms are classic in their beauty, but most guests will be lured out of them by one of the 12 tennis courts, the four Olympic size pools (you can even request a private pool), or perhaps a simple game of ping-pong. Remarkably, the hotel staff members seem to know everybody's name and are always willing to take that extra step to make each guest comfortable. They will be happy to set up a golf game at the Palm Springs Country Club or another private club in the area. Your hosts also encourage you to pick armloads of grapefruit that grow abundantly on the property.

PUPPY POLICIES: Your dog is a welcome addition to the Racquet Club. Please keep him/her leashed and away from the pools.

FRISKY FRIVOLITIES:
* Spend the day on the Salton Sea, where you may enjoy the animals at the National Wildlife Refuge or opt to fish and swim at the State Recreation area. The Salton Sea is 38 miles long and 228 feet below sea level, making it a unique inland saltwater lake.
* Lake Cuhuilla - this is a relatively new lake offering ideal swimming, boating, and scenic picnicking sites. Dogs must be leashed, but

217

will definitely enjoy exploring the many acres.
* The walk from the Racquet Club to the city
  of Palm Springs is invigorating. North Palm
  Canyon Drive is a terrific place for shopping
  and dog- or people-watching.


PEOPLE PLEASURES:
* Golf, golf, and more golf. The staff at the
  Racquet Club will assist you in arranging for
  play on a variety of courses.
* Palm Springs Regional Trap and Skeet Club.
  If skeet shooting is your favorite pastime,
  this is the place for you: (619) 347-4811.
* Palms-to-Pines Highway - This is a 130 mile
  scenic drive that leads you down through the
  desert, up into the mountains, and into the
  resort of Idyllwild.


RACQUET CLUB OF PALM SPRINGS, 2743 North
Indian Avenue, Box 1747, Palm Springs, CA.,
92263.

---

# MOUNTAIN VIEW INN
## Palm Springs

INNKEEPER:    Bob Smith

TELEPHONE:    (619) 325-5281

LODGING:      Eleven rooms

RATES:        Double: $35 - 100.
              No credit cards accepted

The Mountain View Inn is tucked away on a little nook of land that is but two blocks from downtown Palm Springs. Once you step inside the adobe walls, however, the hustle and bustle of the main avenue fade, and you are instantly immersed in the peacefulness of the inn. This single-level, deep grey building with Spanish-tiled roofs, has carved a special niche for itself in a town that seems to double in size with each passing year.

All of the rooms face onto one of the two courtyards where flowers and trees surround two good-sized swimming pools and a jacuzzi. It is an intimate environment, one that is very conducive to getting to know your neighbor. You may wish to spend your time conversing and relaxing near the pools, occasionally venturing into your room for a cool drink.

The charming and tastefully furnished guest quarters have been individually appointed. The smallest, (and in our opinion, the cutest) has been nicknamed the Wicker Room. For those who desire a little more space, there are several suites available, all with either king or twin beds. A few of the many amenities include a large wood-burning fireplace, kitchenette, or separate dining nook. Color televisions and an am/fm radios are always part of the furnishings. Thus, when making your reservations, please indicate which of the special amenities you would like in your room.

The Mountain View Inn is literally set against Mt. San Jacinto. The picturesque surroundings and quiet atmosphere make this an ideal spot to spend a short weekend or an even longer retreat.

PUPPY POLICIES: Small, well-behaved dogs are welcome at the inn for a $5/night fee. The inn is small, so please be courteous and keep your little friend on a leash.

FRISKY FRIVOLITIES:
* The streets, behind Palm Springs, have very few distractions for those who enjoy a quiet stroll. If you are in an exploratory mood, a quick jaunt up to the base of the mountains is both exhilarating and scenic.
* Visit a few of the many Indian canyons in the area. Murray and Andreas canyons are two of the more primitive and less publicized cavernous valleys, while Palm Canyon charges visitors a small admission fee.
* A drive to Joshua Tree National Monument will bring you to picnic areas, hiking trails, and interesting rock formations for climbing. In the spring the desert wildflowers are in full bloom offering a spectacular floral show.


PEOPLE PLEASURES:
* The inn provides bicycles for their guests. Pick one up and go for a spin.
* The Palm Spring's Spa offers people a chance to really unwind. Enjoy soaking in their hot mineral baths, relaxing under the hands of trained masseur or masseuse, or check into their other programs designed to pamper you.
* Treat yourself to an afternoon of shopping, sipping cool drinks, or people watching on the "drive". This is just two short blocks from the inn.


MOUNTAIN VIEW INN, 200 South Cahuilla Rd., Palm Springs, CA., 92262.

# INGLESIDE INN
## Palm Springs

INNKEEPER:       Melvyn Haber

TELEPHONE:       (619) 325-0046

LODGING:         28 rooms, suites, and villas

RATES:           Rooms: $75 - 195,
                 Suite: $195 - 500,
                 Villa: $95 - 250.
                 Credit Cards: AE, MC, and VISA.


    The Ingleside Inn is perfectly located near the base of the San Jacinto Mountains and only a short hop from downtown Palm Springs. The inn is truly a "retreat". As you pass through the wrought-iron gates guarding the two entrances, the "rat race" fades away, and you can begin to concentrate on relaxing in the sunshine amidst the clusters of orange and palm trees. The heated pool, jacuzzi, and gazebo are set among a jasmine covered veranda, green lawns, and beautiful floral garden.

    All of the rooms in this Spanish-style inn are individually decorated in soft pastels, interspersed with bright sprays of color. These tones provide the perfect backdrop for the impressive collections of priceless antiques. In addition to the many luxurious amenities, each room has its own private whirlpool and steam bath to ensure your complete relaxation. You may wish to request a few special features such as a canopied bed or a sitting room with fireplace (the Gaelic translation is ingleside). A light snack and refreshing drink from the well-stocked refrigerator can be enjoyed while basking in the desert sun on your private patio or terrace.

    Each morning you will enjoy a complimentary Continental breakfast. A superb choice for lunch or dinner is Melvyns, the inn's restaurant. It is renowned for its fine cuisine and superb wine list. This is also an understated spot, and a favorite among the celebrity set. Frank Sinatra, Howard Hughes, Rita Hayward, and Marlon Brando have all visited the inn's dining room over the years.

PUPPY POLICIES: Your dog is a welcome addition to the inn. Your host has many dogs of his own (although not on the property) and would like to meet yours. Please tell them you are bringing your "friend" when making your reservations.

FRISKY FRIVOLITIES:
* There are dozens of nearby walking trails, bicycle routes, and parcourse stations around the inn for you and your canine companion to discover.
* Check out the excellent hiking trails in the foothills. One area worth visiting is the Joshua Tree National Monument (870 square miles).
* A stroll through downtown Palm Springs is truly an adventure that even your dog will enjoy (especially after visiting a few of the dog specialty stores).

PEOPLE PLEASURES:
* This is the land of golf and tennis. There is a plethora of places in the area to play both. The innkeeper will be happy to assist you in making arrangements for these, and other sports (bicycling or horseback riding).
* Helicopter (Landells Aviation: (619) 329-6338) or champagne hot air balloon rides (Skysports

Aviation: (619) 340-5545) are well worth the money.
* Enjoy an uplifting adventure on the Aerial Tramway: (619) 325-4227, which will bring you up to the Mt. San Jacinto State Park.

THE INGLESIDE INN, 200 West Ramon Road, Palm Springs, CA., 92262.

---

# MARRIOTT'S RANCHO LAS PALMAS RESORT

## Rancho Mirage

MANAGER:       Paul Corsinita

TELEPHONE:     (619) 568-2727 or (800) 228-9290

LODGING:       Deluxe rooms and suites

RATES:         Double:  $70 - 185,
               Suite:  $295 - 995.
               Credit Cards: All Major.

The Rancho Las Palmas Resort has a simple elegance and charm that aptly fits into any desert lifestyle. This resort is basically dedicated to the sports enthusiast. There are two swimming pools on the grounds, as well as a 27 hole championship golf course, and 25 all weather tennis courts. All of these facilities are set against the beautiful San Jacinto mountains.

From the exterior, these buildings resemble Spanish haciendas. However, once inside, guests will find the rooms are beautifully decorated with salmon or beige colored carpeting, and floral bedspreads to match. Accoutrements include color televisions, am/fm radios, and a terrific selection of personal care products. Early mornings and late evenings are conducive to lounging on your private porch or taking a dip in the hydro-therapy pool.

Rancho Mirage has many fine restaurants (if you want to "hit the town") or you may choose to eat in one of the three restaurants at the resort. One of these, The Sunrise Terrace, overlooks the pool and the mountains. This is an ideal place to meet with friends after a long day of golf, tennis, sunning, or swimming.

PUPPY POLICIES: Your dog is a welcome guest at the resort, provided he/she is of the smaller "lap" variety.

FRISKY FRIVOLITIES:
* There are acres of land and many paths to walk with your little friend. You may wish to use the leash to ensure he/she does not take a dip in the resort's rivers or ponds.
* Bicycle trails and parcourses are close to the hotel. For additional sites, you may wish to check the Palm Springs area.
* Shopping and people watching in Palm Springs in truly an experience. Take your curious canine along and visit one, or all three of the dog specialty stores.

PEOPLE PLEASURES:
* Rent horses at the Smoketree Stables and ride through the desert or into the mountains and canyons: (619) 327-1372.
* Ballooning over the desert at either sunrise or sunset is truly a magnificent and unique experience (especially with champagne).
* Enjoy the many natural scenes up in the high country of Idyllwild, or hike through the Indian Canyons. Visit the botanical gardens and nature trails of the Living Desert.


RANCHO LAS PALMAS RESORT, 41000 Bob Hope Dr., Rancho Mirage, CA., 92270.

# LA QUINTA HOTEL AND RESORT
## La Quinta

MANAGER: Judy Vossler

TELEPHONE: (619) 564-4111, CA:(800) 472-4316, U.S.: (800) 854-1271

LODGING: 268 rooms and suites located in Spanish style cottages

RATES: Double room: $90 - 170, Suite: $195 - 1,300. Credit Cards: AE, MC, and VISA.

La Quinta Hotel's name is derived from the Spanish phrase "la quinta", which means the fifth day. This day used to be particularly special for travelers, as they would ride only a short distance before enjoying great drink, music, dancing, and food. Today, La Quinta still adheres to many of these traditions by subtly striving to accommodate all of their guests' needs. This is achieved with a 1 to 3 staff to guest ratio. Their impeccable standards and attention to detail, are just two of the reasons why La Quinta stands as one of the oldest hotels in the Palm Springs area.

The guest rooms and cottages are scattered among 26 acres of towering palm trees, beautifully manicured grounds, and flower gardens. Complete privacy is a luxury guests can expect during their stay. Each of the accommodations, whether they be the original rooms erected in 1926, the deluxe rooms constructed in 1968, 1982, and 1984, or the superior rooms built in 1981, are very elegantly appointed. The spacious bedrooms are furnished with fireplaces, wet bars, parlors, king-size beds, private lanais, and many other accoutrements.

Guests have several recreational options and facilities to choose from while visiting La Quinta.

Their tennis complex is particularly noteworthy, with 22 championship courts. It is currently rated as one of the top 50 clubs in the United States. There are nine swimming pools and health spas in which to relax after you finish a round or two of golf at the La Quinta Hotel Golf Club.

PUPPY POLICIES: Your small, cosmopolitan dog will enjoy vacationing at La Quinta if he/she will abide by their rules. The management requests that dogs be leashed when strolling the grounds, and should not be left alone in the room.

FRISKY FRIVOLITIES:
* Try some of the terrific hiking in the local mountains, canyons, or on the trails on top of San Jacinto.
* Explore the resort's 800 acres which are set against the mountains.
* Drive over dramatically changing terrain to Idyllwild, where you may enjoy the shopping hiking, or playing in the snow.

PEOPLE PLEASURES:
* Take an elevating ride on the Palm Springs Tramway. This provides an ideal escape to the coolness, spectacular views, and hiking: (619) 365-1391.
* There are miles of trails surrounding the resort for those avid horseback riders.
* Bicycle rentals: (619) 325-7844 are available. Look for the local paths that are marked with blue or white signs.

LA QUINTA HOTEL, GOLF & TENNIS RESORT, P.O. Box 69, 49-499 Eisenhower Drive, La Quinta, CA., 92253-0069

# APPENDIX

AMERICAN FAMILY BED & BREAKFAST
P.O. Box 349
San Fancisco, CA., 94101
(415) 931-3083

AMERICAN HISTORIC HOMES B&B
P.O. Box 388
San Juan Capistrano, CA., 92693
(714) 494-7050

BED & BREAKFAST-CALIFORNIA SUNSHINE
22704 Ventura Blvd., Ste 1984
Woodland Hills, CA., 91364
(213) 274-4494 or (818) 992-1984

BED AND BREAKFAST OF LOS ANGELES
32074 Waterside Lane
Westlake Village, CA., 91361
(818) 889-8870 or 889-7325

BED & BREAKFAST OF SOUTHERN CALIFORNIA
P.O. Box 218
Fullerton, CA., 92632
(714) 738-8361

CALIFORNIA BED AND BREAKFAST
P.O. Box 1581
Sacramento, CA., 95818

DIGS WEST
8191 Crowley Circle
Buena Park, CA., 90621
(714) 739-1669

EYE OPENERS BED & BREAKFAST RESERVATIONS
P.O. Box 694
Altadena, CA., 91001
(818) 684-4428 or 797-2055

HOMESTAY
P.O. Box 326
Cambria, CA., 93428
(805) 927-4613

HOSPITALITY PLUS
P.O. Box 336
Dana Point , CA., 92629
(714) 496-6953

NAPA VALLEY B&B RESERVATIONS
P.O. Box 2147
Yountville, CA., 94599
(Please write for brochure, $1.00 ea.)

SACRAMENTO INNKEEPERS ASSOCIATION
2209 Capitol Ave
Sacramento, CA., 95816
(916) 441-3214

SEA VIEW RESERVATIONS BED & BREAKFAST
P.O Box 1355
Laguna Beach, CA., 92652
(714) 494-8878

WINE COUNTRY BED & BREAKFAST
P.O. Box 3211
Santa Rosa, CA., 95403
(707) 578-1661

HOTEL AND MOTEL CHAINS THAT WELCOME YOUR DO

The following is a listing of hotel and motel chains
in California which, as a general policy, welcome
you and your dog. Please keep in mind that the
ultimate "dog policy" decision is left up to the
individual chain member. For instance there may
be a nightly "pet fee" or size restriction so please
call the hotel or motel of interest in advance for
more specific information.

The following toll free numbers will put you in
contact with each chain's national reservation
service. They will be happy to provide you with
more specific information.


DAYS INN OF AMERICA
1-800-325-2525

HOLIDAY INN, INC.
1-800-465-4329

HOWARD JOHNSON'S
1-800-654-2000

QUALITY INN INTERNATIONAL
1-800-228-5151

RAMADA INNS, INC.
1-800-228-2828

# INDEX

231

# TRAVELING WITH MAN'S BEST FRIEND

If you are unable to find this book in your local
bookstore and wish to receive one or more copies,
please write to the publisher:

DAWBERT PRESS, INC.
P.O. Box 546
Larkspur, Ca., 94943

Please add $ 1.00 for postage and handling.
California residents add 6% sales tax.

TO ORDER: Indicate the number of copies you
would like and print or type the form below.

Make check or money order payable to:

DAWBERT PRESS, INC.

Name _____

Address _____

City _____ State _____ Zip _____

Please send me _____ copies @ $8.95 each.

Please allow 2-3 weeks for delivery.